To

Managing Complexity

WITPRESS

WIT Press publishes leading books in Science and Technology.
Visit our website for the current list of titles.
www.witpress.com

WITeLibrary

Home of the Transactions of the Wessex Institute, the WIT electronic-library
provides the international scientific community with immediate and permanent
access to individual papers presented at WIT conferences.
Visit the WIT eLibrary athttp://library.witpress.com

Managing Complexity

George Rzevski

&

Petr Skoblev

George Rzevski

&

Petr Skoblev

Published by

WIT Press

Ashurst Lodge, Ashurst, Southampton, SO40 7AA, UK
Tel: 44 (0) 238 029 3223; Fax: 44 (0) 238 029 2853
E-Mail: witpress@witpress.com
http://www.witpress.com

For USA, Canada and Mexico

WIT Press

25 Bridge Street, Billerica, MA 01821, USA
Tel: 978 667 5841; Fax: 978 667 7582
E-Mail: infousa@witpress.com
http://www.witpress.com

British Library Cataloguing-in-Publication Data

A Catalogue record for this book is available
from the British Library

ISBN: 978-1-84564-936-4
eISBN: 978-1-84564-937-1

Library of Congress Catalog Card Number: 2014934009

Printed by Lightning Source, UK.

Contents

PART 3   A roadmap into the future   **177**

19   A vision and ideas   **179**

The story of managing complexity   **187**

References   **189**

Authors   **193**

Index   **197**

Introduction

This book is written for those who are determined to prosper under the conditions of a rapidly increasing complexity of the Internet-based global market. It contains an original method for managing complexity and describes many practical examples of the results achieved by applying this method to a variety of business problems.

It will be useful for business executives, administrators, politicians, IT professionals, engineers, scientists and students, who need help in adjusting their mindsets to the reality of a relentlessly increasing complexity of the information society.

It may be also helpful to general readers who are perplexed by the complexity of environment in which we live.

All the case studies described in the book are unique, without precedent, and range from real-time scheduling of 2,000 taxis in London and transportation of crude oil around the globe by 10% of world capacity of seagoing tankers, adaptive cargo delivery to the international space station, semantic processing of scientific abstracts, dynamic patterns discovery from large quantity of data and real-time management of global supply chains, to adaptive management of design modifications to large aircraft wings.

The case studies are backed up with a concise outline of fundamental concepts, principles and methods of complexity science. An insight is provided into the connection between digital technology and the ever-increasing complexity of contemporary social and economic environments and our unique and powerful method for managing complexity is described in some detail.

The book contains an extensive description of the fundamentals of multi-agent technology, which have been developed by the authors and used in the design of complex adaptive software and complex adaptive business processes.

The last chapter provides a glimpse into the future, speculating on the probable consequences of the unstoppable increase in complexity of our social and economic environments and on possible new openings, which may become available to future entrepreneurs.

To help readers to absorb the content, the book is written like a story rather than as a scientific thesis. However the story is based on solid scientific research exposed to scientific community through many publications listed at the end of the book.

The content is a product of over 20 years of joint research, software development and entrepreneurial activities by the authors. Most of our original ideas that have grown into successful practical applications were conceived during informal conversations between the two of us and then implemented by a team of talented software developers under our supervision.

Inspiration for our work was provided by the Nobel Prize winner Ilya Prigogine [1,2], who is generally regarded as the father of the Science of Complexity.

Knowledge contained in this book has been applied to the design and construction of a very large number of adaptive systems, which have added a considerable value to the businesses of our clients and is therefore corroborated by real-world applications.

As a rule, we undertake to solve problems that are too complex to be solved using conventional thinking and conventional technology, problems that frequently change while you are trying to solve them and require a system capable of reacting rapidly and positively to these changes, in real time, and in perpetuity.

To the best of our knowledge there are no other comparable industrial solutions to those that we developed and described in this book.

Acknowledgement

We gratefully acknowledge contributions of our families, colleagues, students and friends, who have helped in this difficult endeavour.

Helen and Vera supported us with love, care and patience throughout many years of hard work, late evenings away from home, and frequent globetrotting to present our research results at conferences, seminars and lectures, or to talk to clients.

Prof. Vladimir Vittikh, previous director of the Complexity Management Institute of Russian Academy of Sciences, Samara, invited George to visit Samara in 1990 to deliver a series of lectures on multi-agent technology to researchers of the Academy. This was George's first trip to Russia and an opportunity to get in touch with his roots and to meet Petr. Vladimir acted as a catalyst and since then, three of us have worked in synergy and forged a lasting friendship.

Special thanks are also due to Bjorn Madsen, who was instrumental in developing our supply-chain expertise and who thoroughly reviewed many drafts of this book.

Elena Simonova worked with us from the beginning and encouraged us to write.

Yana Bogdanova produced all the illustrations for the book, working to an impossible schedule.

We have worked with hundreds of bright and hard-working researchers, software developers and businessmen on conceiving, designing and implementing the commercial multi-agent systems. We acknowledge their innovative efforts.

We are grateful to all who have helped by discussing with us our ideas, providing feedback after our seminars or by making suggestions on how to improve early drafts of this book.

PART 1

Fundamentals

1

What is complexity?

Introduction

Frequent occurrences of unpredictable events create *uncertainty*.

Until recently unexpected changes in our environment occurred rarely and we were brought up by the educational system to expect a stable world operating in a steady state, at least during the lifespan of a generation. We are steeped in Newtonian Science postulating determinism and predictability. We expect that reductionism will triumph and that, sooner or later, a single universal law of physics will explain everything. It is comforting to be able to plan our lives and live to see our expectations fulfilled; uncertainty on a large scale feels menacing. The reaction is often: Let us stop this nonsense. Who is in control? Who is behind this unexpected event that affects me so badly? What is the government doing about it? Is there a conspiracy? And, of course, there are no readily available answers to these questions and nor is there the possibility to stop the world and get off. Some individuals can "give up the rat race" and escape to remote areas, which are not yet affected, but is this the best we can do? What if we all attempt to do it?

Consider for a moment how many important issues we do not know how to resolve. Here are some examples:

- We do not understand the mechanism of global warming.
- All our attempts to eradicate poverty, inequality and crime have, so far, failed.
- We are not sure how to deal with the fact that globalisation increases standard of living across the board, but it also widens the gap between the rich and the poor.
- We spend exceedingly large amounts of money on the "war against terrorism" without visible results.
- Political and/or military interventions aimed at protecting a particular social group often end up causing more harm than good to the very people who we mean to help.

All the issues listed above are *complex*, which means they were not necessarily purposely created or are due to someone's incompetence; they *emerged* as unforeseen consequences of billions of small and large decisions that we all made during our routine daily work. Such issues can only be resolved by the application of a new thinking, thinking that embraces complexity science as recently formalised by Prigogine [1,2] and by the researchers of the Santa Fe Institute, notably, Kaufman [3] and Holland [4,5].

There is another point that must be considered. We seem to be oblivious to the changes occurring everywhere around us and continue with practices, which were successful in the past, forgetting that the environment in which we live and/or work has changed beyond recognition. We should ask ourselves, are these time-honoured practices still relevant to the modern world?

Here are some examples showing our enduring obsession with outdated concepts such as economy of scale:

- We build large computer-based systems, which are, as a rule, delivered late and over the budget, and some never manage to work as expected.
- We still create exceedingly big commercial, administrative or health organisa-tions paying the chief executives huge salaries and bonuses although there is sufficient evidence that smaller organisations are more profitable, customer- and employee-friendly. Do we really need banks that are "too big to fail"?
- We continuously increase the size of schools in spite of the evidence that smaller ones provide better educational conditions and enjoy superior academic success.

Should we not stop for a moment and reflect on Einstein's suggestion that *we cannot solve problems applying the same thinking as when we created them*?

Large systems were cost-effective in the world in which the critical success factor was the economy of scale, the world that was stable and predictable. Recent changes in our environment, in particular, the stepwise increase in the complexity of the markets and of our social environment have rendered large systems less effective, too rigid to adapt to frequent disturbances and, really, not desirable. Shall we ever get Schumacher's message "Small Is Beautiful" [6]?

Wherever we look, in business, in administration, in leisure, the rapidly increas-ing complexity is creating issues, which need to be resolved using new thinking: *complexity thinking*.

The often-quoted statement, attributed to Stephen Hawking at the end of the 20th century, best illustrates the importance of understanding and managing complexity:

> I think the next century will be the century of complexity.

Let us consider the fundamentals of complexity thinking and illustrate how they could be employed to solve complex problems.

Defining Complexity

We all seem to have intuitive notions of complexity and yet there is no generally agreed precise definition. Many researchers in the field of complexity science find this to be a disappointment. On the contrary, this is how it should be. We can never have a precise definition of complexity because, well, complexity is *complex*.

We don't have precise definitions of knowledge, intelligence, emotion or creativity for the same reason, and yet the lack of precision does not prevent us from using these concepts effectively.

Our broad definition of complexity is as follows:

> Complexity is a property of an open system that consists of a large number of diverse, partially autonomous, richly interconnected components, often called agents, has no centralised control and whose behaviour emerges from the intricate interaction of agents and is therefore uncertain without being random.

Key notions here are openness (rich interaction with the environment); diversity, partial autonomy and interconnectedness of agents; lack of centralised control; and emergence.

Complex Versus Complicated

The English language has two similar words that have quite different meanings, namely *complex* and *complicated*.

"Complicated" uses the Latin word "plic" that means, "to fold", while "complex" uses the "plex" that means, "to weave".

A complicated system is folded and thus conceals its internal structure. Nevertheless, given enough time we can discover how it works. We can partition a complicated system into a number of subsystems and if the constituent subsystems are still complicated we can partition each one of them into further sub-subsystems and continue with partitioning until we reach the level at which we can discover its secrets. Behaviour of a complicated system is therefore predictable.

A typical complicated system is not only aircraft, a jet engine, a computer, an algorithm, a monolithic computer program, a mass production line, but also a centrally planned economy, a hierarchically organised corporation and a dictatorship.

On the other hand, a complex system consists of interlinked components that introduce mutual dependencies. It is not possible to proceed with partitioning of a complex system top-down in a fashion described above without destroying it by ignoring some of the links. The behaviour of complex systems is in principle unpredictable because it emerges from the intricate *interaction* of its components. Not from the components themselves, from their relations.

A typical complex system is a cloud, the atmosphere, ecology, climate, the Internet-based global market, a family, a team, a partnership, a swarm of bees, a human being, the human brain, human society, culture, epidemics, a terrorist network, road traffic, a swarm of software agents and the life of aircraft or a car.

It is important to understand that the opposite of complicated is simple and opposite of complex is independent.

Some examples of contrasting complex against complicated systems, as described in Ref. [7], are given in Table 1.

Table 1: Complex versus Complicated.

COMPLEX SYSTEMS	COMPLICATED SYSTEMS
The Internet-based global market	Centrally planned economy
Flexible manufacturing system	Mass production line
Management team	Command and control management
Adaptive scheduling system	Batch scheduling system
Multi-agent system	Large monolithic computer program
Agent negotiations	An algorithm
Aircraft life cycle	Aircraft

Complexity and Uncertainty

Let us use uncertainty as the demarcation parameter to distinguish complex systems from deterministic or random, as shown in Table 2.

The term deterministic implies that uncertainty is equal to zero, whilst the term random means that uncertainty is one. Complex systems have uncertainty value between zero and one.

Table 2 highlights the link between complexity and uncertainty: Uncertainty is a consequence of complexity and it increases with complexity. Low complexity systems have uncertainty close to 0 and their behaviour differs little from the behaviour of deterministic systems. Highly complex systems with uncertainty close to 1 are "at the edge of chaos" and their behaviour is characterised by very unusual features such as self-organisation, generation of unpredictable extreme events and co-evolution.

Table 2: Complex versus Deterministic and Random.

RANDOM	COMPLEX	DETERMINISTIC
Uncertainty $= 1$	$1 >$ Uncertainty > 0	Uncertainty $= 0$
Components have full autonomy	Components (called agents) have partial autonomy	Components have no autonomy
Disorganised	Self-organising Evolving	Organised
Unpredictable behaviour	Emergent behaviour	Predictable behaviour

The Seven Criteria of Complexity

We have identified seven key attributes that distinguish complex systems from deterministic and random [8]: *connectivity, autonomy, emergence, nonequilibrium, non-linearity, self-organisation and co-evolution.*

The Internet-based global market, perhaps the most interesting example of complexity [9], will be used here to illustrate the seven properties of complexity.

Connectivity

A complex system consists of a large number of diverse components, known as agents, which are richly *interconnected*. Connections may vary in strength. Higher connectivity and weaker connections, which can be easily broken and new formed, imply higher complexity. A complex situation is more like a cloud than a structure – there is no clear configuration and clear boundary between the system and its environment.

This is exactly how we can describe the Internet-based global market: it consists of an exceedingly large number of suppliers, consumers, investors, lenders, savers, bankers, etc. who are engaged with each other in trading. Connectivity, and therefore complexity, has increased beyond recognition with the widespread use of the Internet. Strength of the links between players is variable; some are almost permanent (long-term supplier–customer relations), but many links are very weak and they frequently change (some customers tend to change their orders/suppliers frequently).

Autonomy

Agents are not centrally controlled; they have a degree of *autonomy* but their behaviour is always subject to certain laws, rules or norms. Increased autonomy of agents implies higher complexity.

The global market has no central planning or control system and yet the "free market" is anything but free; market participants are subject to national and international laws, regulations, established norms of behaviour and many diverse undeclared pressures. The degree of autonomy of market participants affects the complexity of the market and can be adjusted by varying regulations to increase or decrease complexity as required.

Emergence

Global behaviour of a complex system *emerges* from the interaction of agents and, in turn, constrains agent behaviour. Emergent behaviour is unpredictable but not random; it generally follows discernible patterns (a new order). The emergent properties of a complex system are not present in the constituent agents.

Global distribution of supply to demand emerges from local transactions. It is unpredictable although certain patterns of behaviour can be detected (e.g., boom-bust cycles).

Nonequilibrium

Complex systems generate unpredictable disruptive events. As a rule, systems have no time to return to the equilibrium between two disruptive events and therefore their global behaviour is usually *far from equilibrium*. In cases where a system does manage to return to equilibrium, this will be an *unstable* equilibrium.

Beinhocker [9] states that markets clearly operate far from equilibrium; new transactions get done and previously agreed transactions get changed with such a frequency that the market has no time between two disruptive events to return to equilibrium.

Non-linearity

Relations between agents are *non-linear* (they exhibit properties such as self-acceleration, self-amplification and even autocatalytic properties). Non-linearity occasionally causes an insignificant input to be amplified into an extreme event (butterfly effect). More often, the accumulation of many insignificant inputs over time creates extreme disruptions (drift into failure). The point at which the accumulation of small disturbances is transformed into an extreme event is called the tipping point.

Extreme events in markets are exemplified by the financial crisis of 2008 [10]. Taleb [11] warns that as complexity of the Internet-based global market increases, extreme events may become more frequent and/or dangerous.

Self-organisation

Complex systems *self-organise*, i.e., autonomously change their behaviour or modify their structure, to eliminate or reduce the impact of disruptive events (adaptability) or to repel attacks (resilience). However, after a disruption, a system may not fully recover, and in time its performance may deteriorate (systems tend to "drift into failure") due to the accumulation of small incremental changes.

The drift into failure may be stopped and reversed if constituent agents have propensity to spontaneously initiate self-organising activities aimed at improving performance whenever an opportunity presents itself (emergent intelligence, creativity). Some complex systems are capable of improving their performance by learning from experience.

Perpetual self-organisation is in evidence in the global market as participants react to any disruptive event by changing or cancelling transactions. Creativity is exercised when participants autonomously decide to initiate changes to improve their performance, i.e., by switching to a supplier offering higher quality services.

Co-evolution

If we define the system environment as the set of all systems with which the system interacts, then we can postulate that complex systems are open, they adapt to their environments, and in turn, change their environments. The process is irreversible.

In other words, systems and their environments co-evolve.

Co-evolution of the global economy, technology and society is given in Table 3.

Table 3: Co-Evolution of Society, Economy and Technology.

STAGES IN SOCIAL EVOLUTION	KEY RESOURCES	DISTRIBUTION	SCOPE	SUCCESS FACTORS
Agricultural society Agricultural economy Earth cultivation tools	Land	Village roads	Local	Efficiency
Industrial society Industrial economy Mass production technology	Capital	Motorways and railways	Regional and national	Economy of scale
Information society Knowledge economy Digital technology	Knowledge	Digital networks	Global	Adaptability

Negative and Positive Aspects of Complexity

We are interested in complexity primarily because it affects those who live and work in complex environments and therefore our research is directed towards discovering methods for managing negative features of complexity and taking advantage of features that are positive, from the point of view of those affected.

In general, frequent unpredictable disruptive events and non-linearity are the most difficult aspects of complexity to live with. Disruptive events include ever-changing patterns of demand, supply and competition; changes in previously agreed deals, orders and promises; delays, cancellations, failures and interruptions; security breaches, fraud and hacking (1 billion of attacks were experienced in the fourth quarter of 2012).

Frequently occurring and unpredictable, disruptive events prevent us from sensibly planning our behaviour and acting upon our plans. Businesses and administrations have great difficulties in managing the allocation of resources to demands when the latter are volatile and impossible to forecast correctly.

Even more harmful are extreme events caused by non-linearities in complex systems, such as a global financial crisis, on a large scale, or a sudden loss of an important client, on a smaller scale. A "drift into failure" due to the accumulation of many small servicing and administrative mistakes, which have resulted in at least one airline disaster [12], is a warning to executives and administrators who cannot master a switch to "complexity thinking" in spite of the overwhelming evidence that old paradigm does not work.

Self-organisation and co-evolution are, on the other hand, often considered to be the positive sides of complexity.

Wouldn't it be useful, for example, to belong to a social, political and/or commercial organisation, which is capable of self-organising in reaction to an unpredictable disruption, and eliminating or, at least, reducing consequences of its impact? Spontaneously initiating performance improvements or co-evolving in harmony with its environment?

A further extremely useful feature of complexity is the diversity of agents. It guarantees the survival of species. There are approximately 7 billions of humans on the planet Earth, each one being unique and different from others. No attack, no epidemics will ever destroy all of us – diversity will ensure that the human race survives.

Examples of complex systems where the capacity to rapidly self-organise provides substantial resilience to strong external attacks include epidemics, terrorist networks, human immune system and the Internet.

The relativity of notions "positive" and "negative" is highlighted by the above examples. The attribute of self-organisation for the propagation of a disease or of a terrorist network is positive for the disease and for terrorists, respectively, but is negative for their victims.

Finally, *Complexity is responsible for uncertainty and uncertainty creates opportunities. This book aims at helping readers to exploit these opportunities.*

Evolution Favours Complexity

The interesting questions are where does complexity come from and why are there currently so many complex issues?

There exists compelling evidence that, as the evolution of our Universe takes its course, the ecological, social, political, cultural and economic environments within which we live and work tend to increase in complexity. This process is *irreversible* and manifests itself in a higher *diversity* of emergent structures and activities and in an increased *uncertainty* of outcomes.

The natural selection, which governs evolution, favours adaptability and diversity (and therefore complexity) as winning attributes.

We should learn from evolution. When we design products and services we should consider complexity as a potentially useful attribute and learn how to exploit complexity features such as self-organisation and co-evolution to improve performance of organisations and systems.

We admit that the idea of designing complexity into our lives is counterintuitive and will be very difficult to accept by many. And yet, we have repeatedly demonstrated that when complexity is forced upon us by our environment, the best policy is to manage the situation by developing complex organisations and systems, which can rapidly adapt and eliminate, or at least reduce, consequences of disruptive events that are not under our control.

Co-Evolution of Technology, Economy and Society

Society co-evolves with technology for wealth creation.

The industrial society, where the key resource was capital and the majority of people were employed in the industrial production of goods, superseded the agricultural society, in which the key resource was land and the majority of people were employed in agriculture.

We have now entered a new transition from the industrial to the *information society*, the society in which the key resource is *knowledge* and where the majority of people are employed in knowledge-based services (information processing) rather than in the production of goods.

Co-evolution of society, economy and technology is illustrated in Table 3. Tools aimed at improving the quality of life change economic activities, which in turn change society. Invented tools become available only if the society decides to invest in them and use them.

It is important to note that as the economic system evolves so do the key economic success factors. Economy of scale, the undisputable key success factor during the industrial economy, is less and less important as the complexity of the knowledge economy increases. The new key success factor is *adaptability*, the ability to rapidly produce a constructive response to unpredictable changes in the market.

Complexity and Information Society

Digital Technology as a Driver of Social Complexity

Complexity of social systems advances in steps as shown in Fig. 1. The process is similar to paradigm shifts in science [13].

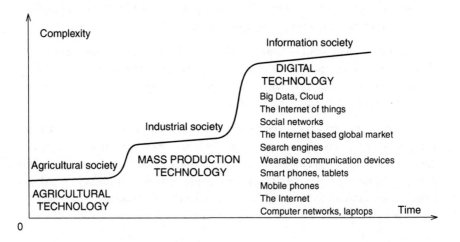

Figure 1: Stepwise increase in complexity of social systems over time.

The current transition from the industrial to the information society, which began after the end of the World War II with the invention of computers, is particularly notorious by the very steep increase in complexity caused by the rapid spread of digital technology, which offers unparalleled social connectivity.

During the transition between the agricultural and the industrial society the increase in complexity was much smaller and yet, in some respects, even more dramatic. The rapid migration of the population from the countryside to the cities to take advantage of new employment opportunities caused well-documented disturbances and, at the same time, increased the social connectivity (due to new social relationships evolved in the increasingly dense cities) and thus complexity. A rigid, traditional social order based on land ownership was replaced by a chaotic transition, which then settled into a new social order based on ownership of capital, only to be shaken again by a new transition to the information society.

During the current transition digital technology has enabled a dramatic increase in social connectivity (social density) but this time without any need for the population to move. Now we can form communities of interests across the globe. Distances do not matter anymore.

Thanks to digital technology, participants in the information society interact faster, more frequently and with greater number of correspondents than ever before. High connectivity, of course, causes high level of complexity.

In 2013 approximately 3 billion people have used the Internet, which is more than 40% of the total number of people on the planet and, according to the TIME NewsFeed, up to 6 billion people had access to a mobile phone – an astonishing increase in complexity caused by the increase in connectivity.

Globalisation

As connectivity increased we have experienced a very important shift from nation-centred industrial markets to the global economy. A recent Organisation for Economic Co-operation and Development (OECD) report showed that globalisation has increased wealth across the board. Economists describe this phenomenon by saying "globalisation tide lifts all boats". Indeed, during the 30 years preceding the momentous financial crisis of 2008, the world as a whole had enjoyed an unprecedented economic growth, with one downside feature – though the poor got richer, the gap between the rich and the poor grew.

The gap in wealth between rich and poor individuals within a country as well as the gap between rich and poor countries is an emergent property of the complex global market. New thinking is required if we want to resolve the issue of inequality.

Shift from Capital to Knowledge as the Key Resource for Economic Activity

In the industrial economy money could buy any knowledge needed for business. In the knowledge economy the *knowledge of how to solve complex problems* can attract investments that are required to start and sustain an economic activity. Pioneers of the knowledge economy, founders of knowledge-based companies such as Microsoft, Apple, Google, Amazon and Facebook are the new economic elite.

Drucker was the first to identify knowledge as the key business resource for the new world emerging after the end of the World War II and the first to coin the term "knowledge worker" [14].

As the complexity of our social environment increases we need new knowledge to resolve new complex issues – a strong incentive indeed to invest into the education of innovative minds. And we have at hand digital technology, which is eminently suitable for collecting, storing, processing and distributing Knowledge (the key resource of the information society) and is the only technology whose performance-to-cost ratio is continuously increasing.

Shift from Mass Production to Production for Individuals

As individuals improved their living standards and acquired new means of communication, which enabled them to broaden their horizons, they began asserting their individuality by demanding customised products and services. The trend is unmistakably present in many walks of life, including switching from packaged to individually tailored travel and in the creation of new opportunities for specifying and ordering customised products and services over the Internet.

The new trend of demanding personalised products and services fundamentally changed the way suppliers planned production and run supply chains. In many industries the end of mass demand has signalled the end of rigid resource planning and batch processing.

Our entrepreneurial activities started when we were invited by one of the largest and most successful car manufacturers in Germany to advise on how to deal with an unfamiliar situation: their dealers, prompted by orders from individual customers, started to change specifications of options for cars previously ordered in bulk, at least once every 2 hours, whilst their production planning systems required at least 8 hours to produce an optimal production schedule and therefore could not cope with the new dynamics of demand. The obvious solution was to get rid of the ERP (enterprise resource planning) systems working in batch mode and to introduce adaptive schedulers capable of rapidly rescheduling in real time the affected parts of the production whenever a disruptive event occurred. However, in 1999 such a solution seemed too radical.

Shift from Manufacturing to Knowledge-Based Services

The shift of mass manufacturing from the developed to the developing countries is a part and parcel of globalisation. The replacement of mass manufacturing by knowledge-based services as the main wealth creation activity may be achieved only in the countries where there exists expertise in advanced information technology (IT) and a large number of high-class knowledge workers: researchers, designers and decision-makers in financial services, IT, engineering, consulting, construction, architecture, entertainment, media, etc.

The knowledge-based services encompass all services that are the product of intellectual work, as exemplified by research, product and service design and development, marketing and selling, prototyping, development of manufacturing technology, project management, problem solving, software development, IT services, architectural design and construction supervision, provision of business services, consulting services, publishing, news industry, entertainment industry, investment management, banking, health care provision, education, training, human resource management, logistics services, and etc.

Most of these services are well established rather than new. What is new now is the cost-effective technology for digitising, storing, processing and transmitting knowledge, which enabled trading in knowledge across the continents.

The early adoption of knowledge-based services provides an excellent opportunity for economic prosperity at the time when the mass manufacturing focused countries face stiff competition.

Advanced manufacturing is a different story. Research and design, which provides competitive advantage to manufacturers such as Rolls Royce, Airbus, Boing, Mercedes, Bosch and Dyson, is an *extremely important knowledge-based service*. Knowledge created by this service is then packaged into advanced materials by manufacturing processes. The key value of the manufactured end products is the knowledge rather than the packaging.

Apple, Google, Facebook and Microsoft, on the other hand, package knowledge created by researchers and developers into software, rather than into physical goods. Quite naturally, businesses, which wrap their knowledge into software, print or as advice, achieve substantially higher value added than do manufacturers, who must purchase expensive materials and/or components externally.

It will be interesting to monitor how new innovations (e.g., 3D printing and electric cars) are going to change the economic landscape.

Shift from Big Corporations to Digital Enterprises

Big monolithic corporations are the product of the industrial economy, which was characterised by stable markets generating steady demands for identical, mass produced goods. Big corporations were designed to be rigid and permanent and they thrived in the era when the economy of scale was the key success factor.

The new complex global market is the enemy of anything big and rigid. The new critical success factor is adaptability and therefore we can safely assume that large corporations will not have an easy future, with the exception of those that manufacture uniform products exemplified by nappies or nuts and bolts.

However, big corporations have a remarkable ability to survive and many will reinvent themselves and continue in a more appropriate format.

The organisational structure that is most suitable for delivering to perpetually changing markets is a network of self-contained production units, each having a unique expertise (knowledge resource), often referred to as virtual enterprise [15].

Virtual enterprise is a network of interconnected autonomous units, each unit being an organisation or individual. Links between the units may be autonomously and dynamically established, dropped and re-established depending on the enterprise needs (self-organisation). There is a considerable uncertainty as to capacities required for non-core activities and therefore each virtual enterprise tends to have a partnering arrangement in place with a larger number of companies or individuals than absolutely necessary (strategic redundancy of resources), just in case that some of them will be busy when their services are needed. Since all the semi-permanent partners operate in the same highly volatile environment, it is in their own interest to be interconnected with many potential purchasers of their services. As competitive conditions change over time, virtual enterprises may permanently drop connections with some of the old constituent units and seek to establish links with new units (evolution). Virtual enterprises typically co-exist and compete/collaborate with other virtual enterprises and since they are all trying to improve their performances in respect to each other concurrently (co-evolution), they create an ever-changing environment. Not every enterprise gets its game right – there are always companies, which underperform and those that disappear. New companies are formed and they join the market and compete for the requisite number of connections. Global economy performs as the natural ecology.

There is a real possibility now for large corporations to reorganise themselves internally into virtual business units and avoid the destiny of planned economies. The popular name for this transformation is digital enterprise.

Shift from Face-to-Face to Online Retail and Banking

Transition is gradual and it is most likely that both types of retail and banking will persist well into the future. Nevertheless, the savings that retailers and bankers can achieve by expanding the Internet-based operations are substantial and the transition will accelerate.

The shift from face-to-face to the internet-based retail has many unexpected implications, not least the "long tail", "the wisdom of crowds" and "economy of attention" phenomena, which are described in the following sections.

Long Tail
In the economy based on selling goods from physical retail outlets, because of a high cost of floor space, retailers can afford to store only those goods that sell well,

as represented by normal distribution with short tails. Businesses selling over the Internet don't have this disadvantage because they can store goods at distant and cheap locations or order the goods when required without ever storing them, and therefore they can make large profit by selling goods that generate high margins, although they sell only in small numbers, i.e., goods that are under "long tails" of a normal distribution [16].

The Wisdom of Crowds

Experiments show that, on average, the opinion on any subject of a large number of people randomly selected (large crowd) is remarkably similar to opinions expressed by experts [17]. Therefore, the Internet-based retailers can expose their goods and services to very large audiences and can invite them to review their offerings without needing to hire experts.

Economy of Attention

At conferences conducted in halls and in lecture rooms the speakers have guaranteed full attention of their audiences, whilst if the same content is displayed on the Internet, there is no guarantee that anybody will notice it. Information providers have to fight for attention of visitors to the Internet [18].

Shift from Face-to-Face to Online Education and Training

As a natural consequence of the emergence of global knowledge economy (economy in which the key resource for economic activity is knowledge), the demand for knowledge and therefore for higher education will continue to rise. It is likely to accelerate.

Many countries will find the transition into an information economy difficult and will experience hardship in one way or the other. There will be a great need for knowledge workers and severe shortages of funds to expand higher education provision.

Digital technology will help – it can cost-effectively process, store and deliver educational material and, perhaps more importantly, provide support for *interactive independent learning* and *communication of ideas*. It promises to substantially reduce the cost of education per student and, arguably, improve the quality of education by switching control of the learning process from teachers to learners, with teachers retaining the important role of learning facilitators and advisors.

Trend drivers outlined earlier will enable a large proportion of the world population to pursue a lifelong education through courses offered by a variety of virtual universities, i.e., geographically distributed university-centred consortia or partnerships, often on a global scale, interconnected by digital networks such as the Internet.

Emergence of the Digital Leisure Industry and Social Networks

The current shift from paper-based and analogue media to digitally enabled entertainment as the main leisure activity was made possible by the astonishing progress in designing miniature and powerful processors and memory chips, and appropriate communication and application software, as evidenced by the rapid spread of multichannel digital TV, digital cameras, cellular phones and digital audio and video devices. This is complemented by a rapid growth of websites for downloading and uploading art, music and multimedia products. Apple iPod, iPhone, iPad and iTunes together with Google, YouTube and Facebook are the icons of this revolution. The spread of social networks, where individuals display their creative efforts to be perused by global audiences, is particularly significant and certain to continue well into the second half of this century.

Personal Globalisation

Through the specialised websites it is now possible to outsource many personal tasks such as search for dating partners, personal secretarial tasks, personal website design, bookkeeping for freelancers, private maths coaching for students and graphic design for weddings. The outsourcing provides opportunities to take advantage of better value for money, e.g., services of a college graduate in India for $15 per hour (versus $60 per hour in the USA), maths coaching from Bangalore for $99 per month or graphic design from Argentina for a wedding at $65 per job; but also, to reduce inequality of knowledge workers around the globe by providing freelance work at a distance for those in developing countries.

Big Data and Knowledge Discovery

As available computer storage space is increasing relentlessly and the Internet enables sharing of data, there is a trend to accumulate exceedingly large quantity of data – Big Data – and store it on extensive server farms, referred to as Clouds. Data is used to improve intuitive judgements of experts with extensive data mining aimed at discovering useful patterns in data [19,20], which amounts to using computers to discover knowledge, the key resource of information society. Data mining is used extensively in marketing to individual consumers but also in unexpected areas, which include football coaching, medical diagnosis and in teaching – discovering which teaching methods work with which individual student.

The Prospect of Semantic Web

The next technological revolution will be the shift from the current data-driven Internet to the new Semantic Web and it is likely to be dramatic, as the new generation of systems will be enabled to interpret the meaning of data. Semantic Web is an old dream of computer science researchers, which is now on the way to be realised with first programs based on ontology and multi-agent software being released and tested in commercial applications [21,22]. Further progress is ensured by the concentrated effort of a large number of researchers in EU and the USA.

Functionality required to implement Semantic Web is fundamentally different from that offered by the current software technology. Clarifying semantics of sentences expressed in a natural language requires intelligent computational effort rather than brute force of current software.

Threats from New Forms of Violence

With the rapid increase in the number of people connected to the Internet and/or travelling across the globe, new global malevolent complex systems have emerged, such as terrorist networks, global epidemics, massive hacking attacks, phishing and spamming. It is an unpleasant and dangerous side of the Internet revolution, which, in turn, provides the opportunity for creating a wide variety of early warning and security systems. Co-evolution of attacking and defending systems will continue well into the future.

Digital Democracy versus Digital Big Brother

The concentration of data on credit card transactions, on communication with friends and business associates and on individual mobility in huge Clouds, by organisations such as Google, raises important questions on individual privacy. It is only natural to expect that those who have knowledge about us will try to use this knowledge to manipulate our behaviour.

Knowledge is power. Who will exercise this power acquired by accumulation of digital data about every aspect of our life?

Will a private company (possibly in collusion with a government intelligence service) manage to acquire sufficient quantity of data to establish monopoly of knowledge? Or, can we expect that the process of natural selection will ensure the distribution of knowledge?

We are optimistic. As we said before, evolution favours complexity, which imply diversity and distributed decision-making rather than centralisation, although the transition is by no means smooth.

Complexity and Philosophy

Two Competing Worldviews

For a long time eminent philosophers and scientists, among them Aristotle, Kant, Newton and Einstein, have maintained that the world is inherently deterministic. Created by the "grand design", our Universe behaves in a predictable way and any uncertainty that we may experience is due to our lack of knowledge. As we learn more we reduce uncertainty. Finally, a universal law will be discovered that will enable us to explain and predict everything (reductionism).

A part of this worldview is the belief that complexity is the name we give to things that we do not understand and that with increased understanding complex things become simple.

An alternative worldview was formulated recently by Prigogine [1]. The world is inherently complex (unpredictable but not random). It self-organises and evolves with time. Its evolution is irreversible.

The future is not given – it is under perpetual construction. The future emerges from the interaction of billions of current activities, natural and artificial.

Some elements of this worldview were present in teaching of Buddha and Heraclitus, who famously wrote "No man ever steps in the same river twice", circa 500 BCE, and much later in publications of Faraday and Popper.

Darwinian evolution is the major scientific contribution to this worldview.

Now let's consider practical implications of each of these two worldviews.

Determinism

If we believe that we live in a deterministic world then for every *effect* there must be a *cause* and therefore for every ill effect there must be a culprit. It follows that somebody must be responsible for poverty (a good candidate is a greedy capitalist) and for a global financial crisis (greedy bankers, who else?) and for riots (left-wing agitators?) and for unreasonable strikes (irresponsible unions?) and for everything else, of course, there is a cause.

The cure is always very simple: decision-makers must make sure that every possible outcome of their decision is properly investigated, consequences predicted and the best outcome selected using ethical and rational criteria.

Another premise of determinism is that the reality exists objectively, independently of us, and we can observe and make models (simplified representations) of the objective reality.

Complexity

On the other hand, if we believe that we live in a world in which a very large number of diverse agents interact in a non-linear way, and the world unpredictably and irreversibly evolves as a result of billions and billions of actions performed by these agents, it is not possible to identify a culprit for any misfortune. As a rule, we are dealing not with a single cause, we have many insignificant inputs that may be amplified and may accumulate over time to reach a tipping point and cause a catastrophic event; or cancel each other.

Issues such as poverty, financial crisis and even riots and strikes are emergent properties that are too complex for "cause–effect" analysis. Complex issues emerge from the interaction of agents; they are not a result of a single agent failure (although such a failure may be a contributing factor).

In a complex world decision-makers cannot, in principle, identify all possible outcomes and, even less, predict consequences of their decisions with any precision.

Detached, objective observation is not possible. No observer can observe without interfering. Our perception of reality is subjective, coloured by local information. We have no way of knowing what reality really is. We cannot see "the big picture", it changes perpetually, it evolves.

Switching the Mindset

Most of us were brought up believing in determinism, whilst to succeed in a modern world, which recently arrived uninvited, there is a need to understand complexity. The switch is necessary but difficult and the resistance by those who made it in the yesterday's world is passionate, exactly as described by Kuhn [13].

What exactly is the complexity mindset? Here are some elements:

- Accepting that the world in which we live and work evolves and that we have to adapt to changes in our environment.
- Giving up hope that we shall be able to identify precisely unique causes of our successes and failures.
- Consenting that organisations slowly "drift into failure" and that it is necessary, from time to time, to inject into them innovative ideas, methods, services or products, to reverse the drift and improve their performance.
- Understanding that with every decision and action we actively contribute to construction of our future and therefore shortcuts are not acceptable.
- Learning that time is a precious resource and that all decisions and actions will have to be performed in real time.
- Expecting that uncertainty of outcomes hides opportunities, which are there to be discovered.

2

A method for managing complexity

To the best of our knowledge, the method of managing complexity described in this chapter is our original contribution to the art and science of prospering under conditions of complexity [8,23,24]. The method has been tested on numerous practical applications, some of which are described in Part 2, invariably yielding economically viable results.

Introduction

If we accept that "to control" means to specify a desirable behaviour of a system and to steer the system towards achieving it, then complex systems cannot be controlled. The very concept of "emergent behaviour" precludes controllability.

Let us establish what else we cannot do.

We cannot eliminate uncertainty by simplifying complex situations. Any change in connectivity would change emergent behaviour of the system in an unpredictable way. If we attempt to impose rigid structures on complex situations, these structures will, sooner or later, break down (remember centrally planned economies?).

We cannot rely on sophisticated mathematical prediction methods to tell us the future. If future is not given, we cannot predict it. However, because complex situations are not random, we can find probable patterns of future behaviours.

We cannot expect rigid planning to work under conditions of frequent occurrence of unpredictable disruptive events. Under such conditions plans soon lose any connection with reality.

What can we do then?

The best we can do is to *manage complexity*, which means to *cope* with external complexity and *tune* internal complexity.

Coping with External Complexity

Coping with complexity is defined here as a means of achieving desirable results under conditions of complexity that is not under our control (in other words, complexity of the environment in which we live and/or work).

The ability to cope with external complexity is very important, for example, for businesses that sell to global markets.

The best strategy for coping with complexity is to develop a capacity for self-organisation that will overcome or at least reduce consequences of disruptive events when they occur, in other words, to become *adaptive*.

As we said in the previous chapter, building the capacity for self-organisation into systems in which we live and work amounts to designing complexity into our life, which is counterintuitive. Common sense suggests we should attempt to simplify the complexity of the environment, which, of course, is not practical because by definition our environment is not under our control.

Tuning Internal Complexity

Tuning complexity is a process of modifying certain parameters of the complex system, which is under our control with the aim of decreasing or increasing its complexity.

Methods for tuning complexity are particularly important for those in charge of complex systems, e.g., authorities that regulate financial services, health care, education, law and order, security and fraud detection as well as managers in charge of business processes such as logistics.

By experimenting with multi-agent models of complexity, we have identified key sources of complexity to be *connectivity, connection strength and autonomy of constituent agents*.

The identification of sources of complexity is of great importance. It enables us to measure complexity and, in cases where we have a power to vary agent connectivity, inter-agent connection strength and agent autonomy, gives us a method for tuning complexity.

Connectivity

The connectivity of agents denotes the degree to which an agent is connected to other agents in the system. If an agent is not connected to any other agent, its connectivity is 0. If an agent is connected to every other agent in the system, its connectivity is 1. In complex systems agent connectivity (C) is in the range of $0 < C < 1$.

The higher the connectivity of agents, the greater is complexity of the system.

Complex systems are by definition (see seven criteria of complexity) highly interconnected, which is an important reason for the uncertainty of their behaviour.

Strength of Connections

Strength of connections between agents denotes the degree of breakability of connections. The lack of connection has value of 0. The permanent connection has value of 1. In complex systems the strength (S) of inter-agent connections is in the range of $0 < S < 1$. Weaker connections are easier to break and make new connections, the feature that increases complexity and, therefore, the unpredictability of global behaviour.

The weaker the inter-agent connection, the greater is complexity of the system.

Weak connections that can be broken when the system self-organises to adapt to an event are an essential attribute of complexity. Strong connections resist self-organisation and very strong connections may prevent system from self-organising.

Autonomy

Autonomy of agents denotes the degree of freedom given to them to decide what to do. If an agent has no freedom of decision, its autonomy is 0. If an agent has full freedom to decide what to do, its autonomy is 1. In complex systems agent autonomy (A) is in the range of $0 < A < 1$.

The higher the autonomy of constituent agents, the greater is complexity of the system.

In complex systems the autonomy of agents is always restricted.

The relation between the connectivity and autonomy of agents, when the connection strength is kept constant, is shown in Fig. 2.

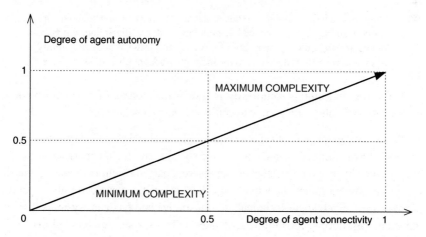

Figure 2: Dependence of complexity on the degree of autonomy and connectivity of agents, when connection strength is constant.

The relation between the inter-agent connection strength and autonomy of agents, when the connectivity is kept constant, is shown in Fig. 3.

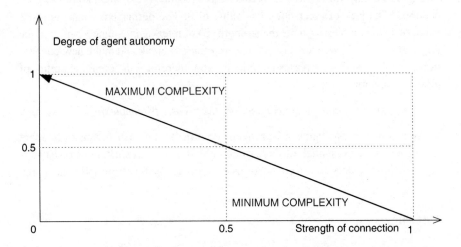

Figure 3: Dependence of complexity on the degree of autonomy of agents and strength of inter-agent connections, when connectivity is constant.

Our experiments with models of complex systems show that:

> Greater agent autonomy, higher agent connectivity and weaker connection strength, i.e., greater complexity, foster creativity, improve adaptability and resilience and increase the speed of recovery after extreme events.

On the other hand,

> Restricted agent autonomy, reduced agent connectivity and greater connection strength, i.e., reduced complexity, enforce discipline, improve predictability, reduce probability of mistakes and fraud, reduce probability of extreme events, reduce creativity and reduce adaptability and resilience.

It follows that tuning complexity is a delicate process of balancing various complexity attributes with a view to achieving desired behaviour.

Whilst we cannot do much about complex physical and chemical systems, which are guided by natural laws, and about some social systems (like marriages), which are governed by social norms that are an inherent part of a culture (social norms do evolve but we don't know how to change them at will), we can certainly affect the behaviour of social, socio-technical, administrative and business systems that are guided by law, norms, constitutions, statutes, policies, rules and regulations.

Emergent behaviour of such systems can be kept within certain limits (attractors) by ensuring that regulations are sufficiently unambiguous to prevent random behaviour and yet sufficiently flexible to allow system certain freedom to experiment when facing new challenges. Experience shows [10] that:

> The best strategy is to introduce variable regulations – tighter when the system operates in a normal mode and much looser when the system is recovering from effects of an extreme event.

It is interesting to note that this research conclusion is directly opposite to what those in charge attempted to do before and after the worldwide financial crisis of 2008.

Regulations cannot prevent system non-linearities creating occasional extreme events. To reduce severity and frequency of extreme events we must tune agent connectivity and, possibly, adjust strength of connections between agents. It is often necessary to ensure that certain parts of a system are more complex than the others. To achieve uneven distribution of complexity over a network it is necessary to organise agents in regions, with high internal connectivity within each region and a sparse connectivity between regions, as shown in Fig. 4.

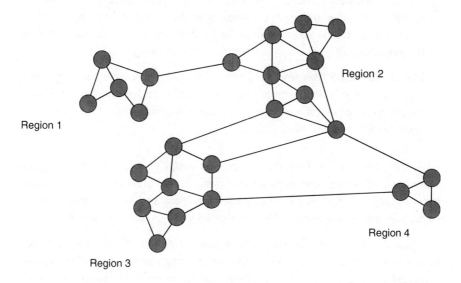

Figure 4: Partitioning a large network into regions prevents propagation of extreme events.

Low connectivity ensures that instabilities cannot propagate between regions whilst high connectivity inside regions enables high regional adaptability. Increasing the strength of inter-regional connections and weakening the strength of internal connections within regions may also help. By redesigning financial services networks in this manner we would impede propagation of instabilities created in one region to other regions.

There exists a widespread misconception that complex systems cannot be designed. This is not correct. The design of complex systems is however quite different from the design of complicated systems; it is less precise and the final outcome cannot be predicted, only projected. Tuning complexity is an important part of designing complex systems.

Modelling Complexity

There are conceptual difficulties in defining modelling if the situation, which is being modelled, is complex, and therefore without clear boundaries, characterised by emergent behaviour, never in equilibrium, with non-linear relations between agents, self-organising and evolving.

Modelling of complex "reality" is definitely more art than science. Our long experience in modelling of complex business situations and processes is outlined below. There are two key rules:

1. Models must have *requisite complexity*. Models of complex systems must be capable of adapting to changes experienced by the system that is being modelled, and the adaptation must be autonomous (without waiting for instructions from the modeller), which is only possible if *models are complex*.

2. Models must have *requisite granularity*. For example, if we model a transport business, it will be sufficient to assign an agent to each truck, but if we study the maintenance of transportation resources, it would be necessary to assign an agent to each component of a truck.

The key implication of this thesis is that current-generation computer programs cannot be used as models for complex situations because they are not adaptive. They cannot change by themselves – they must be instructed to do so by programmers. At present, only multi-agent software technology can support adaptation.

There are many complex issues where constituent components and their inter-actions can be identified and modelled by constructing a network model of requisite complexity and granularity. Most business situations and many social, economic, security and technological problems, as well as the evolution of urban systems, fall into this category. We refer to such issues as large-scale complex.

Once a suitable virtual world is constructed in complex adaptive software, it could be used to simulate behaviours of a complex issue in the real world under different states of its environment, e.g., studying behaviour of a supply chain under varying market conditions [25].

Complexity of certain unresolved critical issues (such as global warming, poverty and population growth) is so high that we can expect, at best, to build much-simplified models of these issues with a view to gaining some insight into their resilience to our attempts to resolve them. Let us refer to such issues as exceedingly complex issues. Exceedingly complex issues nevertheless can be successfully modelled. A brilliant work on modelling of the population growth is done by Kapitza [26].

Our investigation of systemic failures leading to the current worldwide financial crisis [10] belongs to the category of modelling exceedingly complex issues.

Adaptability

There is evidence, as discussed in Chapter 1, that complexity of the world in which we live and work will continue increasing, at least in the near future.

We assert that for organisation and individuals who plan to survive and prosper under conditions of complexity, it is essential to become *adaptive*.

We can rephrase this assertion by saying that adaptability is the key success factor for all who operate in the Internet-based global market, which is characterised by frequent occurrence of unpredictable disruptive events.

Adaptive Allocation of Resources

All problems discussed in this book have been formulated as *the allocation of resources to demands*, as this is one of the most difficult issues to resolve under conditions of complexity.

We have classified resources into:

- Human (e.g., airline pilots, crew, service engineers, insurance assessors, software developers)
- Physical (e.g., machines, transport, storage, plants, buildings, land)
- Financial (e.g., working capital, investments, payment of invoices)
- Knowledge (e.g., patterns discovered in data or text)

ERP systems, which were developed for industrial economy characterised by stable market, work in batch mode (which was appropriate when the economy of scale was a key critical success factor) and handle human, physical and financial resources, without any reference to knowledge as a business resource.

ERP systems are still the most important software component of every current enterprise although market conditions have changed beyond recognition.

It is our assertion that for enterprises that deliver to the current highly complex global market the allocation of resources must be adaptive and must include knowledge as a business resource.

Seven Criteria of Adaptability

From our experience in delivering adaptive systems for the allocation of resources to industry and administrations we have distilled the seven critical attributes of adaptability.

1. Real-Time Decision-Making

Monitoring of disruptive events and deciding how to deal with an event before the next one occurs is done in real time, which means before the next disruption occurs. This usually involves rescheduling of the previously agreed allocation of resources to demands between two consecutive disruptive events.

2. Delayed Commitment

After the decision on dealing with a disruptive event has been made, the implementation of the decision (sending of the new schedule to affected agents) is delayed as long as practical in order to allow time for schedule improvements. Due to repeated adaptations, complex systems tend to experience a deterioration of performance, often called "a drift into failure" and it is therefore necessary to design agents with propensity to initiate self-organising processes aimed at performance improvement and, by means of a delayed commitment, to ensure that there is a sufficient time for these processes to be performed.

3. Minimising Consequences of Disruptions

Any rescheduling required to absorb or neutralise a disruptive event is limited only to the affected demands/resources.

4. Distributed Decision-Making

Constituent agents are empowered to allocate resources to demands by a process of negotiation. Distributing decision-making and coordinating decisions by negotiation, rather than by controlling organisations top-down, ensures that requirements and preferences of all stakeholders are taken into account even when they are in conflict; the emergent final decision is based on trade-offs and conflict resolutions.

5. Anticipation

The future cannot be predicted but we can anticipate it. The trick is to employ the dynamic forecasting of disruptive events, where the term "dynamic" indicates that forecasts are regularly updated by taking into account actual occurrences of events.

6. Experimentation

In adaptive systems decision-makers are given opportunities to experiment with novel methods for improving performance under conditions of frequent occurrence of disruptive events, whenever required.

7. Learning from Experience

An effective way of learning from experience is to dynamically discover patterns linking decisions to performance.

Adaptive Strategy

The key element of adaptability is *adaptive strategy*, a strategy that acknowledges the need for adaptation to complexity of the working environment, identifies complex features of the environment, outlines behavioural options conditioned on probable futures and sets procedures for adaptive behaviour.

An important part of adaptive strategy is to establish a blueprint for an *enterprise knowledge base* and to plan *strategic redundancy* of resources, an appropriate reserve of resources to support a variety of options, some of which may never be implemented, a feature that is important when one cannot predict which resource will be required and when.

This notion is in conflict with a generally accepted wisdom of designing "lean business processes" and "just-in-time" production. Adaptability requires a certain surplus of resources, just in case.

Note that the above attributes are equally effective when the system is electronically attacked (fraud or terrorism). Therefore an adaptive system is by definition *resilient* to fraud and electronic attacks.

Adaptability can be achieved only by employing advanced technology. The scope of the problem and required speed of decision-making are beyond human capabilities. Software technology eminently suitable for implementing adaptability is described in the next chapter.

Conventional IT is not capable of supporting adaptability. Current schedulers and optimisers cannot handle dynamics of contemporary markets; they are designed to start from scratch whenever a change in data is detected and need hours to find the optimal operating point, which becomes obsolete even before it is computed.

Designing Adaptive Business Processes

We outline here a method applicable to the design of any adaptive business process: supply chain, production, transportation, distribution, advertising, servicing, as well as project management, which we have used for the last 15 years to design practical adaptive solutions for industry.

Assuming that an adaptive strategy is in place, the design begins with building a business process knowledge base.

Building a Knowledge Base

Conceptual knowledge is best represented as ontology, a network whose nodes are classes of objects, defined by their attributes and scenarios, and links are relations between classes of objects.

Ontology, in fact, represents a conceptual model of the business process.

For example, for an adaptive airline seat booking and flight scheduling process object classes include flight, passenger, aircraft, pilot, maintenance, seat price, route and network. Examples of attributes include for the object class "flight": flight number, take-off airport, landing airport, take-off time, check-in time, etc.

Scenarios specifying agent behaviour are means of controlling autonomy of agents. If agents are expected to behave according to a single scenario, in other words, a single algorithm, their behaviour will be deterministic and adaptability of the business process will be reduced; a choice of scenarios and an option for agents to experiment when suggested scenarios do not match the reality increases adaptability of the business process.

Factual knowledge, such as lists of concrete resources and demands, may be stored in conventional databases.

The next step is to build an instantaneous network model of the real-world domain that is being investigated, known as *scene*, consisting of instances of object classes and their relations, as specified in ontology.

For an airline, a scene will be a network in which nodes are Passenger P1, Passenger P2, ..., Flight F1, Flight F2, ..., Seat S1, Seat S2, ..., Aircraft A1, Aircraft A2, ..., and links are "S1 is allocated to P3", "A1 is allocated to F2", etc.

Complex systems, such as supply chains of large international organisations, and scenes that represent them may contain millions of objects, attributes, rules and relations.

Constructing a Virtual World

Virtual world is a world of agents, small computational objects, which achieve their tasks by exchanging messages with each other; by interacting.

An agent is assigned to each node of a scene, in other words, to each object instance. For example, in a virtual world of the airline scheduling system, we have flight agents, aircraft agents, pilot agents, airport agents, parking position agents, etc.

Virtual worlds are designed to make real-time decisions through inter-agent negotiations, to delay commitments as long as practical, to assure that only parts of the system affected by an event are modified and to monitor and anticipate the occurrence of disruptive events.

Complexity of the virtual world can be varied by modifying the strength of connections and connectivity of agents as described in the next chapter.

Advanced virtual worlds contain knowledge agents capable of learning from experience by discovering patterns linking agent decisions with successful or less successful past behaviours.

Connecting Virtual to Real Worlds

The real world (i.e., a complex situation that is being modelled) is perpetually changing. The changes are represented by the occurrence of disruptive events.

For an airline, disruptive events may be seat booking, flight departure, flight delay, flight cancellation, airspace closure, aircraft failure, etc.

The occurrence of every real event must be communicated instantly to the virtual world where an equivalent virtual event is created, causing the affected part of the virtual world to adapt to changes originated in the real world.

Every change (adaptation) of the virtual world must be communicated to the real world in time for its implementation.

Empowering Virtual World to Manage the Real World in Real Time

Agents from virtual world decide how the real world should adapt to a disruptive event.

For example, if a real aircraft breaks down, its model, a virtual aircraft also breaks down. The aircraft agent responsible for this node sends messages to agents of all affected nodes letting them know that this virtual aircraft does not exists for a time being. The message provokes a flurry of activities among affected agents who try to accommodate the failure by searching for a replacement. As soon as a solution is found, it is conveyed to the real world for implementation, ensuring that the two worlds co-evolve (change in unison).

It is important to note that once a suitable virtual world is constructed in software, it could be used not only to manage the real world but also to simulate behaviours of the real world under different states of its environment, e.g., studying behaviour of a supply chain under varying market conditions (Fig. 5).

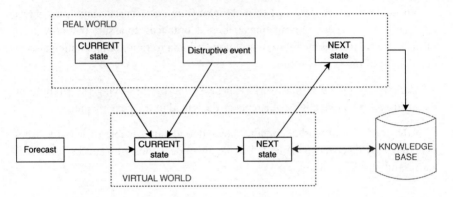

Figure 5: Empowering virtual world to manage real world.

3

Multi-agent technology

Introduction

Multi-agent technology is the key software technology for managing complexity. This chapter provides main concepts, principles and methods of this technology in such a way that it could be easily understood by readers without programming knowledge.

Fundamentals

An agent is a software object capable of :

- Consulting knowledge base to ascertain what is necessary to achieve and how
- Interpreting information found in knowledge base or received from other agents
- Selecting from a set of options the action, which maximises enterprise value
- Composing meaningful messages
- Sending messages to other agents or humans

Agents are activated by disruptive events. They also have propensity to proactively seek to increase enterprise value whenever possible.

Enterprise value is a composite measure of enterprise performance, which includes one or more categories such as profit, service quality, risk containment, complying with various client preferences and is normally different for each enterprise.

Agents always work in swarms (teams, groups).

A swarm of agents comprises several agents competing or cooperating with each other with the aim of accomplishing a common task in a way that maximises enterprise value.

Swarms behave like agents: they react to events, communicate with other swarms, make decisions and act upon them. The behaviour of a swarm emerges from the interaction of constituent agents.

Swarms are assembled into multi-agent systems (MAS). Each swarm may be given a self-contained task or a single task may be partitioned and distributed to swarms.

An MAS is a system consisting of one or more swarms of agents competing or cooperating with each other with the aim of accomplishing a common task in a way that maximises enterprise value.

MAS behave like swarms and their behaviour emerges from the interaction of constituent swarms.

MAS exhibit all features of complex adaptive systems, and in particular, the self-organisation, which, in the context of agent technology, can be defined as follows:

> Self-organisation is the capability of a swarm of agents to autonomously modify existing and/or establish new relationships among its constituent agents with the aim of recovering from a disturbance and/or maximising enterprise value.

We design our MAS specifically to perform adaptive allocation of resources, where demands for resources and/or resources that need to be allocated change during the allocation process in unpredictable manner.

In a typical system, which allocates resources to demands, there will be *demand agents*, *resource agents* and an *enterprise agent*. The task of demand agents is to attract recourses that are required to meet demands, the task of resource agents is to attract demands that can utilise resources, and the task of the enterprise agent is to ensure that the allocation maximises enterprise value. All types of agents are equal and can achieve their tasks only through a process of negotiation with other agents, or humans.

In the context of the allocation of resources any autonomous change of a demand–resource link is considered as a step in self-organisation.

We shall consider here two examples of adaptive allocation of resources:

Logistics – the allocation of transportation resources to transportation orders in time and space, under conditions of uncertainty created by frequent occurrence of unpredictable disruptive events.

e-Commerce – the allocation of available goods or services (supply) to customer requests (demand) when customers and/or suppliers unpredictably join or leave the allocation process.

MAS for Adaptive Resource Allocation

Let us assume that an MAS is given a task of allocating n resources to m demands.

Each resource is characterised by

- A set of f attributes
- Its value expressed in monetary units (mu)

Each demand is characterised by

- A set of g attributes
- Its purchasing power expressed in monetary units (mu)

Typically, demands arrive to the system one by one. Times of arrival of demands and their characteristics are unpredictable.

Resources may be constant or changeable in time.

The allocation process is then as follows:

1. An agent is allocated to the demand as it arrives to the system. The demand agent sends a message to all agents assigned to available resources stating that it requires a resource with particular features and that it can pay for this resource a particular number of monetary units.

2. All agents representing resources with specified features, or with some of the specified features, with the value smaller or equal to the specified number of purchasing units, offer these resources to the demand agent.

3. The demand agent selects the most appropriate resource from those on offer.

4. If no suitable resource is free, the demand agent attempts to obtain a resource, which has been already tied to another demand, by offering to that demand compensation.

5. The agent allocated to the demand to which the offer of compensation is made considers the offer. It accepts the offer only if the compensation enables it to obtain a different satisfactory resource *and*, at the same time, increase enterprise value. If it accepts the offer the demand agent, effectively, reorganises the whole system – the previously established relationship between that demand and a resource is destroyed and a new relationship between a different demand and the released resource is established increasing enterprise value – a clear example of self-organisation.

6. The above process is repeated until all resources are linked to demands and no change of ownership of resources can increase enterprise value or until the time available for allocation is exhausted.

7. Before any action agents consult knowledge base to find out what options are open for them to pursue.

Example of Self-Organisation in Logistics

Let us consider an example from the domain of airship cargo transportation, where there exists (a) a network of loading/unloading sites, (b) routes between these sites and (c) two airships transporting cargoes along these routes (Fig. 6).

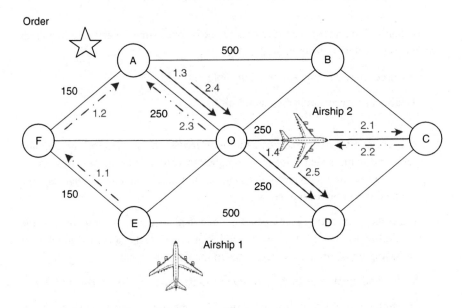

Figure 6: A network of sites and routes (the figures show distances).

One of the two airships has a greater cargo capacity (100 tons), but it is slow (10 km per hour); its operating costs are quite high at 7 monetary units per km (mu/km).

The other airship has a smaller cargo capacity (10 tons), but its speed is higher (15 km per hour). Its operating costs are 3 mu/km.

Situation 1: On 15 September the system receives an order for the transportation of a 5-ton cargo from point A to point D (500 km distance) for 15,000 mu. The deadline is 20 September. Airship 1 is free and located at site E, while Airship 2 is transporting a previously accepted order to site C.

To plan the operation, Order 1 Agent is created. The Agent sends a request with details of the required cargo transportation to both airships. Having considered the request, each airship sends its proposal to the Order 1 Agent.

Airship 1 is ready to start the transportation immediately. To accept the order the airship needs to move from site E to site A (300 km). The cost is $(300 + 500) * 7 = 5{,}600$ mu/km and the time required for the execution is $(300 + 500)/10 = 80$ hours, i.e., about 4 days.

Airship 2 will have to complete the current transportation task first and then move to the site A to undertake the execution of the new order execution. If Airship 2 is currently located at point O, it will need to cover the route O–C–O–A. The time required for the execution will be $(250 + 250 + 250 + 500)/15 = 83.3$ hours, i.e., also about 4 days, and the cost will be $(250 + 250 + 500) * 3 = 3{,}000$ mu. The gross margins of Airships 2 and 1 will be 12,000 and 10,400 mu, respectively.

Given that other conditions are equal, Order 1 Agent will choose the airship that maximises enterprise value, in this case, brings to the transportation company the greatest gross margin, i.e., Airship 2, despite the fact that it will take it longer to get to point A. As a result of this decision, the first link in the network was created between an order (Order 1) and a resource (Airship 2) as depicted in Fig. 7. The link 5 indicates that Order 1 has booked Airship 2.

Situation 2: Let us assume, that 1 hour later, a new order for a cargo transportation was received by the system: 8-ton cargo needs to be transported from point C to point B (150 km) for 20,000 mu. The deadline is 17 September. Order 2 Agent is created to handle this task.

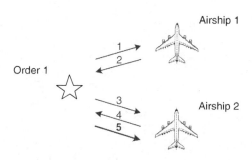

1 – enquiry sent by Order 1 Agent to Airship 1 Agent
2 – proposal sent by Airship 1 Agent to Order 1 Agent
3 – enquiry sent by Order 1 Agent to Airship 2 Agent
4 – proposal sent by Airship 2 Agent to Order 1 Agent
5 – booking of Airship 2

Figure 7:   Order 1 finds two available airships and books Airship 2.

It is clear that only Airship 2 can execute this order: Airship 1 would not be able to meet the deadline, as it would need $(500 + 300)/10 = 80$ hours, or about 3.5 days. In contrast, Airship 2 would need only $(250 + 300)/15 = 36.6$ hours, or about 1.5 days. Yet, Airship 2 has already been booked by Order 1.

In this situation, the enquiry from Order 2 Agent to Airship 2 Agent produces a chain of negotiation:

- Airship 2 Agent sends a message to Order 1 Agent requesting the permission to be released from previously accepted booking with a view to accepting Order 2 and offers unspecified compensation for breaking the previously fixed booking.
- Order 1 Agent attempts to oblige. It contacts the airships again (6) and receives from Airship 1 the same proposal (7), which meets its deadline, and was previously rejected as the more expensive (10,400 versus 12,000).
- Order 1 Agent asks Airship 2 Agent (8) to compensate the difference (1,600).
- Airship 2 responds (9).
- Order 2 Agent considers the request for compensation passed to it by Airship 2 Agent. If it gets Airship 2, its profit will be $20,000 - (250 + 300) * 3 = 18,350$. Therefore, the compensation to be paid to Order 1 Agent is considerably smaller than the profit, which Order 2 Agent will make from the deal. Order 2 books Airship 2 (10).
- Airship 2 confirms booking (11) and is ready to execute Order 2.

These examples illustrate how autonomous self-organisation of a swarm of agents enables adaptation to unpredictable disruptive events.

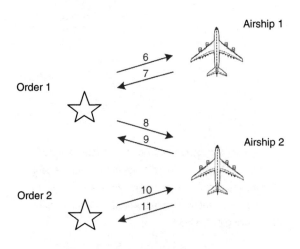

Figure 8: Order 2 re-books Airship 2.

Example of Self-Organisation in e-Commerce

Let us consider an example of selling cars over an Internet portal by an international network of dealers in Germany and Brazil with their own warehouses and transportation means for the delivery of cars. An agent is assigned to each order, dealer, warehouse, transportation unit, transportation slot, transportation load and car. These agents are capable of not only selling cars (which agents of existing e-commerce systems also can do), but of acting very flexibly in the dynamically changing environment, increasing the network gross margin and meeting requirements of all customers, owing to their capability to cancel contracts, reconsider them or change parameters of existing contracts with buyers' and sellers' permission.

Order 1 is for a red Mercedes cabriolet for 50,000 mu to be delivered in Brazil. The car has already been paid for and is now 300 m from the customer's house, being delivered by a truck. The customer has been waiting for it for 1 month already.

Another customer in Germany is planning to get married in 2 weeks and wants to have exactly the same car for the wedding. Dealers in Germany could not find such a car in their warehouses. The system will now try to generate for Customer 1 an alternative proposal, which would be difficult to reject, with a view to delivering the red Mercedes to Customer 2.

To achieve this goal, Order 2 Agent will send a message to Car 1 Agent with an offer of unspecified compensation to induce it to change the customer. Car 1 Agent, in turn, sends a message to Order 1 Agent asking for permission to change the customer.

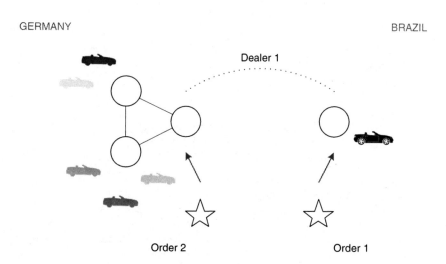

Figure 9: The network of dealers, orders and cars in warehouses.

In response, Order 1 Agent considers the situation and possible solutions, proceeding from its own and the car owner's interests. First of all, it will turn to the Brazilian dealer to find out how fast it would be possible to deliver a new car with the same parameters. Let us assume a new car is possible to deliver within a month, doubling thus the waiting period for the first customer. In accordance with the simple strategy of proportional compensation, Order 1 Agent asks Order 2 Agent for a 50% discount to compensate for the doubling of the waiting period. To obtain permission for the deal, Order 1 Agent contacts Customer 1, say, by sending a message to his mobile phone and offers 50% discount in exchange for the agreement to wait another month. If Customer 1 agrees to wait another month, Order 1 Agent cancels the booking of Car 1 and books Car 2. Order 2 Agent, in turn, books Car 1 for the price which now equals its initial price plus the amount of compensation, $50,000 + 25,000 = 75,000$ mu.

Now, Order 2 Agent has to agree with Lufthansa the delivery of the car back to Germany within 2 weeks. Let us assume that Lufthansa agrees (even if the flights have been fully booked, the enterprise agent can negotiate with agents representing other big loads to give up their transportation slots in return for compensation). All compensations taken into account, the delivery of the car back to Germany will cost 4,000 mu and the full cost of the car will be $50,000 + 25,000 + 4,000 = 79,000$ mu.

This price will be offered to Customer 2, who will receive the negotiation report and see the decision tree (with the urgency of his order taken into account). He can either accept this offer (in this case the truck with the car will stop 200 meters from the house of Customer 1 and will make its way back to the airport) or reject it (in this case, all achieved agreements will be cancelled and the initial situation will be restored).

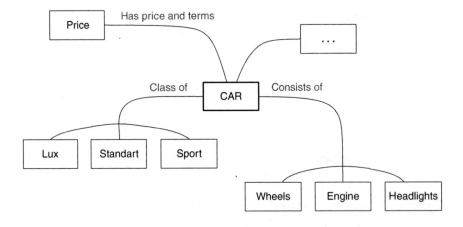

Figure 10: A fragment of car production ontology.

Note, that if both orders are executed successfully, agents gain additional profit by meeting the demands of each participant of the deal (Customer 1, Customer 2, Lufthansa, factory, dealers). Agents achieve this by changing relations between the market participants: by reselling the product, which has already been sold; by the dynamic allocation and reallocation of resources. This example also shows that for full flexibility of e-commerce, there should be no fixed prices and no fixed terms of delivery: everything should depend on customers' requirements.

Knowledge Base

A knowledge base contains all domain knowledge, conceptual and factual, required for agents to negotiate decisions.

Ontology is a part of knowledge base containing conceptual knowledge represented as a network of:

1. Object classes

2. Relations between object classes

3. Attributes of object classes

4. Scenarios (scripts) of object class behaviours

Object classes are nodes and relations are links between them. Together with attributes and scenarios, object classes and relations contain all knowledge elements required for running an MAS.

For example, production ontology will include the specification of ordered products, types of products, time needed for their production, necessary components and conditions and costs of storing components in warehouses.

The discount calculation scenarios can include the following strategies: "*regular customer*" (depending on the number of previous purchases), "*wholesales*" (depending on the purchase volume), "*purchase with delayed delivery*" (the customer pays in advance but can wait for the delivery for certain time), "*competitors' prices*" (making the product price comparable to or lower than competitors' price). There are also other decision-making rules stored here, e.g., rules of resource allocation profitability estimation and estimation criteria defined by users.

A current state of the virtual world at some moment of time is called a *scene*. Scenes may be stored in conventional databases.

Virtual World

The virtual world is a medium where the allocation of resources takes place. Let us consider the simplest virtual world supporting the allocation of resources to demands without reference to time and space, as in e-commerce. In such a world an agent is allocated to each resource and each demand. Demand agents and resource agents negotiate among themselves with a view to achieving the best possible allocation.

Agents in the virtual world may be free (no relations with other agents), in which case, they seek to establish relations with other agents by matching themselves with potential partners (as Yin and Yang or opposite electrical charges). Unattached agents, within the virtual world, have propensity to search for suitable matches, consider the profitability of available matches and make proposals to potential partners.

The relation is established only if the potential partner agrees. The agreement will be granted only if the proposed relation is the best currently available.

The agent is "satisfied" (which will show on its "face") if the match found is better than average for the given market or, in some cases, if the match is for full value, and "dissatisfied" otherwise. The agent's dissatisfaction is a reason for reconsidering the established relation at the first opportunity.

If, having searched the market, an active agent finds no suitable match, it switches to a passive state and waits for a message from other agents or for the occurrence of an event capable of changing the scene, e.g., a new request for resources arriving to the system causing the creation of a new demand agent. On the occurrence of such an event, the agent becomes active. It returns back to a passive state when the negotiation chain, generated by the event, is over. Agents, which have established relations with other agents (achieved matching), may also switch to a passive state: they switch on their timer and wait for the initialisation. In logistics, for example, component agents passively wait for the component delivery to the conveyor.

When agents are activated by a message, the process follows the following sequence. Free agents are activated first, dissatisfied agents second and satisfied agents are activated last (to reconsider their links on the basis of the method of compensation, if needed).

Let us consider the agent interaction using a simple example depicted in Fig. 11. There are seven agents keen to perform matching and establish relations with each other. Demand agents are shown in white, resource agents are in grey. Two agents to the left have already established a relation (the solid arrow between them) and are satisfied by their link – they have smiling faces. The three agents in the centre also have smiling faces: they are in the process of making decisions and establishing relations (the broken arrow). The group to the right are in the process of decision-making but are not pleased with the conditions at all (they have sad faces) they probably do not see a good match possible. Note that either order agents or resource agents can be active (as the arrows show).

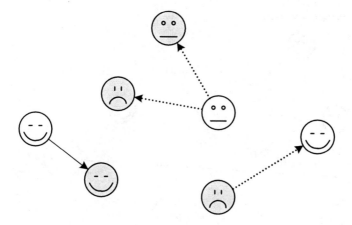

Figure 11: A scene: matching of demand agents (white) and resources agents (grey).

As a rule, agents can abort relations only by mutual agreement. But there are exceptions, which we shall discuss later.

In simple virtual worlds described so far, there are no rules except for the rules of communication.

To solve logistics problems it is necessary to consider additional factors, namely space and time. The implication is that it is necessary to construct a map of locations of sites and routes (highways, air and sea routes, etc.) with its dimension and scales, as depicted in Fig. 12, and place there warehouses, conveyors, transportation resources, etc. It is also necessary to consider at what time the allocation of a resource to a demand should be accomplished.

Every scene is defined by panels of agents and relations in terms of doubly linked lists, which allow the processor to proceed from every agent or relation to its neighbour. Elements of these lists refer to each other: this allows agents to find their relations and thus agents, with whom these relations have been established. In practice, these agent and relation panels are also divided into panels of active and inactive and satisfied and dissatisfied agents in order to reduce the processor time for searching the execution queues at the system dispatcher.

Decision-Making

The decision-making unit is a set of procedures and data structures, which considerably simplify the execution of decision-making scenarios. These procedures are written in a special language capable of handling the basic data structures and actions, such as organising information exchange among agents, collecting information about supply and demand dynamics, finding possible connections between

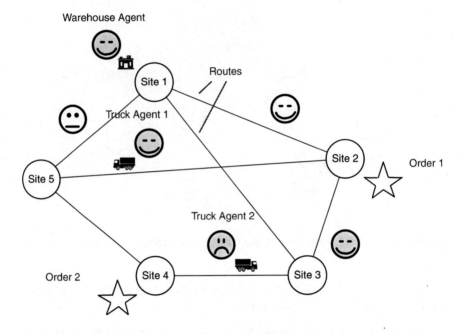

Figure 12: A scene in a logistics world.

agents, selecting the best connection, executing decisions and reconsidering them if the situation changes.

Each agent is described by a list of its properties and their values as follows: <Property 1 = Value 1>, <Property 2 = Value 2>, ... To learn about agent properties and their values, agents can exchange messages (do you have such a property? what value is defined for it?).

To simplify the scenario logic and reduce the number of requests, some properties can be "invisible" to other agents. The decision-making is performed on the basis of the information collected from messages, defined a priori and contained in the world model and rules of agent behaviour in different situations. The world model defines which agents of which classes can be found in this world, what relations they can have and what actions can be performed on them.

The typical data structure for decision-making is a table of offers with information about received proposals. An example of such a table for a demand agent in logistics is depicted in Table 4. To make it simple, the table shows only three properties: product class, costs and time of delivery.

The structure of the table will vary, depending on how many properties have been defined for the demand and resource agents. The basic table operations of the virtual decision-making machine are creating/deleting the table, defining or

Table 4: Typical Decision-Making Table.

No.	Offers	Product Class	Cost	Time of Delivery	Agent's Gross Margin	System Gross Margin

clearing fields, sorting offers according to a field and searching for a string using patterns.

The most important step is to choose the best offer. This procedure can be very complex. The simplest case is when there is a full matching possible between demand and supply (e.g., in price and time of delivery). A more complex case is when demand and supply are close to each other as measured by an agreed metrics (partial matching).

To accomplish matching between demand and resource properties the demand agent can send a request, indicating or not the rating of properties and their values: "are there any A class resources with value Z1 for property A1, importance B1, and with value Z2 for property A2, importance B2?", etc. Resource agents check resource properties and their values in ontology and respond. Even if they do not match those indicated in the request, resources can be offered as possible candidates for partial matching.

There are two ways to perform the priority-based demand–resource properties matching:

1. *Sequential matching of properties, starting with top-priority properties.* The first demand agent sends a message to resource agents: "I am class N Demand Agent. If there are any class N Resource Agents with name S1, specify your value". After it receives their replies, the demand agent creates a "property–value" table. From the table it chooses one or more suitable offers and sends to their agents the question: "Do you have property S2? If yes, then what value does it have?" This strategy allows the agent to proceed from more important properties to less important; apply the partial matching strategy (e.g., not paying attention to properties of minor importance); reduce the number of comparing operations; keep its closed property values hidden, changing them in accordance with its negotiation strategy or market situation (e.g., number of competitors).

2. *Parallel matching through a mediator.* Demand agents disclose their open and hidden properties to a mediator, who calculates indexes and returns them to agents. Agents do not know exact values of other agents' properties but are aware of the degree of their similarity or difference as indicated by indexes.

Table 5: Market Indicator Table.

No.	Product	Current Average Price	Increase or Decrease

Another important data structure for decision-making is the market indicator table, which shows the average supply and demand indexes. Table 5 plays an important role in agent negotiations.

Agent Negotiations

Agent negotiation is an important mode of decision-making. Negotiating, agents change and coordinate their actions and agree on transaction values (if this is allowed). For example, if a resource price equals its production cost + storage costs + 10% profit, then the agent responsible for this resource can reduce its profit to, say, 5%, to make the product price lower than the price offered by its competitors.

There are different ways of implementing negotiation strategies within the system logical architecture. The most common method is peer-to-peer (P2P) negotiations. The other way is to organise a virtual round-table for agents to negotiate on the "many-to-many" principle, which is effective when a large number of agents need to agree on each decision.

Observing the virtual world scene, each agent in turn makes a proposal and other agents check proposals according to their system of values before responding. If some constraints are exceeded (e.g., the project budget), the negotiation returns one or several steps back to find an alternative path and the process continues.

Architecture

The architecture of our MAS at the highest level is shown in Fig. 13.

Main modules are described in the following sections.

Knowledge Discovery Module

Knowledge discovery module discovers useful patterns (knowledge) in data, which can be used for demand forecasting or for the analysis of state of repair of resources, etc. For example, if a big order is coming every Friday it is reasonable to book specific resources for implementation of this order tentatively in advance. And if the order has not arrived as expected the customer can be alerted and/or resources can be released.

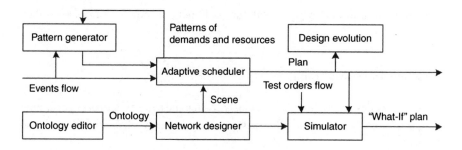

Figure 13: MAS architecture.

Adaptive Scheduler

Adaptive scheduler processes the flow of disruptive events and creates schedules in real time, giving user opportunity to interactively adjust schedules.

Ontology Editor

Ontology editor helps to build or edit ontology of a network, which is required for constructing specific scenes of networks. Ontology contains classes of objects and their relations, attributes and behaviours. Examples include for objects (truck, factory, cross-dock, etc.), relations (resource "is booked" for a demand), attributes (value of an order) and behaviour (business processes).

Scene Editor

Scene editor configures the enterprise network and describes the initial state of the network manually or automatically, extracting data from different sources (databases, XLS or XML files, etc.). For this purpose the user needs to select and load appropriate ontology, which is used as a dictionary of concepts and relations in the process of specifying the concrete customer network. If concepts and relations required to specify the new network are not available, domain ontology needs to be expanded using the ontology editor.

Simulator

Simulator is the tool for playing what-if games. At any moment the current state of the supply-chain network can be loaded on to simulator to answer various questions like, for example, what will happen if a new big orders arrived unexpectedly. Another option is to reconfigure the network (changing geography of main resources or making a new type of equipment available) and to run different scenarios of network optimisation in parallel with the continuous scheduling of orders as they arrive.

Evolutionary Design Module

Evolutionary design module autonomously creates and evolves networks generating suggestions on how to adapt the network to perpetually changing demand and supply.

The architecture of the central component of the above system, the scheduler, is shown in Fig. 14.

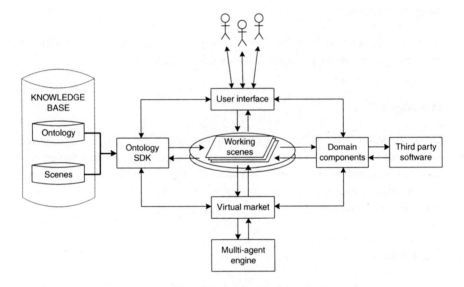

Figure 14: Architecture of our adaptive scheduler.

Main components of the scheduler are outlined in the following sections.

Ontology

Ontology is structured as a network that describes knowledge on how the virtual world works containing both declarative and procedural components. Within a virtual world described in ontology, populated by physical and abstract entities, one can create scenarios for performing actions on constituent objects and their responses, in accordance with rules imported from the corresponding section of the real world. For example, for an order agent the logistics ontology would describe what items are needed to complete the order, who produces or delivers these items, and who can order and receive them. The details of the transaction are not coded; they are separated into text files to be automatically edited. If high efficiency of the system is needed, simple agents are utilised. There is also a need to describe abstract worlds, e.g., the world of logistics (which includes objects such as order, schedule and deadline, etc.) and the world of business (which includes objects such as profit, income and business transaction). In the process of constructing a scenario, it is possible to define parameters for objects and agents and to set their initial states (e.g., for a warehouse or a transport system) and to enter initial orders. Then, the virtual world can be set in motion.

To speed up the work of a system, some parts of the ontology can be hard-wired by developing libraries of extensions of the run-time system. With respect to the basic libraries of the system and in accordance with certain rules, objects (including the basic types of agents) and methods that can be called by agents are constructed. They can be programmed into the system or called in at the run-time. In a critical case, to increase the efficiency of the system, the whole subject domain ontology can be implemented as a selection of objects and methods of a library of extensions.

Virtual World
The virtual world is a model of a domain of the real world. It is a space in which agents perform their tasks cooperating and/or competing with other agents.

Engine
The engine is a virtual parallel machine for running virtual worlds and supporting concurrent operation of agents, a subsystem for communication support, modules for ontology support, the dialogue management subsystem and the service subsystem.

Interface System
Having loaded a virtual world, the user can construct different scenarios describing how this world works, using the interface system. For example, in the logistics system, in a virtual world for an enterprise, a user can place on the screen cities and roads, assembly lines, group technology cells and means of transport. A virtual market for an enterprise can be built for agents to trade and to develop contracts.

The main user interface window of the scheduler allows importing orders and placing them in the queue, starting planning and reviewing the schedule using a Gantt chart and map, including detailed information about journeys and key performance indicators (KPIs). Different parts of the window can be easily configured and rearranged. At any moment users can view agent inspector showing which agents are currently working in the system.

To check how agents made allocation decisions users can analyse agent negotiation log.

Multi-Agent Platform

To avoid coding every new application from scratch it is advisable to identify components of MAS that are present in the majority of applications and to configure them into a system referred to as platform. To develop a powerful platform capable of supporting industrial applications it is necessary to have a considerable experience in designing, implementing, commissioning and maintaining a variety of multi-agent applications.

A platform should include support for all components as shown in Figs. 8 and 9.

Our platform is continuously evolving to reflect experience gained through developing applications. We describe here several components of the MAS engine, which is a constituent part of the platform.

The Subsystem for Running Parallel Processes

This subsystem enables control of a very large number of agents compared with the standard thread mechanism. Switching control from one process to another is organised by including in the program special interruption points as system calls. There are versions for working with ontologies and for direct coding of agents.

The Subsystem for Extending the Engine with Functions of Dynamic Loading/Reloading Modules of Extensions

This mechanism allows a programmer to add to the system new modules of extensions: both for developing the functional part of the system, including new basic types of agents, and for the system interface (graphs, dialogues).

The Subsystem for Support of Ontology

The principal task of this subsystem is to provide access to ontology. This subsystem is a link between the description, generated by the ontology development toolkit, and the system.

The Subsystem for Translation and Execution of Scripts

Scripting languages are an important part of ontology that allows the description of complex parallel scenarios for agents and for linking them to specified preconditions.

The Subsystem for Communication

One of the principal features of agents is their ability to communicate with other agents. Great attention has been paid in the engine to the mechanism for messaging. The mechanism allows a programmer to send messages in both synchronous and asynchronous modes; to accumulate queues of messages for each process; to detect messages sent to discarded agents and to provide a log of messages for debugging agents' interactions.

The Subsystem for Serialisation/De-serialisation in the Context of Agent Work

This mechanism provides a unified saving/restoring of scenes of agent states, in the process of simulation of agent work in real time. The mechanism allows the interruption of all processes at any time to continue their work later.

The Subsystem for Linking with the External System of Visualising/Control

This subsystem allows the use of any external system, coded in accordance with specified requirements, to activate the engine.

Main Features of Our MAS

Our view is that multi-agent technology is technology, which can be conveniently used to build complex adaptive software. Indeed, adaptive resource allocation systems that we build using agent-based software, and which are described in Part 2 of this book, satisfy all seven criteria of complexity.

To ease building complex adaptive software using agent technology, we have developed a number of original tools, which are described in the following sections.

Extended Ontology

Our ontology, in its most comprehensive version, contains scripts for agents to guide them how to achieve specified goals (e.g., how to compose a message and how to interpret received message). As a rule, agents have a set of alternative scripts from which to choose, what to do, as well as rules (some of which may be contradictory) to guide them which script is appropriate in which situation. If an agent encounters a new situation, which is not covered by a script, the agent may be allowed to experiment by sending to affected agents a tentative proposal what to do and modify the initial proposal taking into account comments received from other agents.

In the most advanced versions of ontology, rules controlling autonomy of agents as well as scripts specifying agent behaviour can be modified by users during system operation, without needing to recompile the system.

Requisite Granularity

When you model a real-life situation one of the key decisions is to determine granularity of your model, in other words, to determine what is the smallest component of your model. For example, if you model a supply chain, should the smallest component of your model be a warehouse or a position on a shelf in a warehouse.

In the context of MAS, this translates into a decision, which will be the smallest object in your model that will be represented by an agent. This decision is crucial because it determines how many agents your model will have to handle.

To help with this decision we introduced the concept of *requisite granularity*, i.e., the granularity that is necessary to have in order to perform adaptive allocation of resources to demands. For example, if we model a car rental business, the smallest components of our model will have to be rental orders and rental resources, i.e., rental reservations, cars and drivers delivering cars. For modelling the intercontinental network of car rental stations, the granularity can be much coarser – the smallest object class can be a car rental station.

Virtual Microeconomics

To achieve the best possible allocation of resources to orders in a volatile environment, agents representing orders are given certain amount of *virtual money* to enable them to pay for required resources and charges are imposed on the acquisition of resources with a view to creating free market trading conditions; to speed up the reallocation caused by the occurrence of an unpredictable event, *virtual taxes* are levied on each transaction, which decreases the number of incremental changes caused by an event.

An important part of microeconomics is the concept of *enterprise value*, which expresses the sum total of desirable achievements for the enterprise and may include profit, market penetration, costs reductions, service quality, customer satisfaction and well-being of members of the enterprise.

The fundamental principle of microeconomics is that if a new order cannot find a suitable free resource it may make an offer to a previously engaged resource promising to pay a compensation for the annulment of its previous match. Such an offer may trigger a wave of negotiations, including negotiations for the release of the resource from its previous allocation and the acquisition of a new resource by the abandoned order. The wave of matching and rematching may extend to several previously agreed allocations.

Virtual money available for the payment of compensations in this chain of nego-tiations comes from the budgets of agents that ask for renegotiation. In exceptional cases where an order comes from a VIP customer, an additional sum of virtual money may be released by the enterprise agent to ensure that the privileged order is fulfilled, even on expense of the overall enterprise value.

For certain applications there is a need to speed up the agent negotiations and for this purpose the method of *compensation* is replaced by *drop-and-go* method, which allows newly arrived orders to grab a resource previously allocated to another order without compensation (or a limited compensation) provided this transaction increases the enterprise value.

In situations characterised by frequent disruptive events, the rematching of orders and resources in real time (between the two subsequent occurrences of any significant change) substantially increases enterprise value, which is not the case with simpler incremental methods, where orders are matched to resources on the first-come-first-served basis, or via auctions.

Agent Satisfaction

Agents can find in ontology the value of objects that they represent and can deduce if this value has been realised in transactions that they negotiated. Satisfied agent is an agent that has fully realised the value of the object that it represents (in some cases, if the realised value is above average for the current market) and partially satisfied agent is an agent that has realised this value only partially. Satisfied agents have a propensity to defend the allocation that they negotiated, whilst partially satisfied agents have propensity to find a better match for their objects.

Here is an example. If a taxi driver agent is assigned a customer that travels in the opposite direction to the direction to which the driver wants to travel, the agent will be only partially satisfied and will start proactively searching for a "better" customer. On the other hand, if a driver agent is allocated a customer, who travels in the same direction in which the driver prefers to travel, it will be fully satisfied and will resist any requests from other driver agents to give up its customer unless it is offered a substantial compensation.

This feature helps to improve enterprise value by giving priority in any rescheduling to partially satisfied agents.

Demand and Resource Proactivity

Proactivity is one of the key conditions for effective teamwork. One can hardly imagine a productive team where everyone is passive and makes no contribution unless specifically asked.

Similarly, agent proactivity turns to be very important in improving enterprise value. For example, when truck agents are only partially satisfied with their assignments, they can proactively seek other options by offering their services and proposing discounts to order agents. Agents of trucks which are almost fully loaded may recapture the initiative and proactively seek those orders that would make the trucks fully loaded. The same applies to previously allocated orders, which are not active for some reason (e.g., orders that belong to a group).

When a resource successfully attracts orders, which were previously allocated to other resources, this change initiates a ripple effect of renegotiations, which in turn increases the enterprise value.

Proactivity can also be directed towards the external world. The system can propose to the operator to accelerate or postpone delivery of certain cargoes in order to increase the enterprise value. For example, if an order due tomorrow can be profitably delivered today, then this option should be offered to the customer even if he did not ask for an early delivery.

Proactive interaction with customers (approved by company managers), that takes into account the enterprise interests in the developing situation, may also increase enterprise value.

Enterprise Agent

We have introduced the enterprise agent into our virtual world to look after global interests of the system, or to rephrase it, to maximise enterprise value.

If the enterprise agent finds that one or several parts of the schedule contain weak links, it may initiate the process of destruction and rebuilding of those parts of the schedule. The reconstruction may be based on changed goals of agents participating in negotiations to enable them to form improved structures, for example, starting with minimisation of costs and proceeding to reducing risk. To accomplish this task, a new group of agents is formed for a certain period of time. If the reallocation does not produce an improvement, the previous schedule can be restored.

This method is similar to the method of random disturbances used to improve decisions in classic numerical optimisations, but due to a combination of top-down and bottom-up strategies, this method turns out to be more flexible. Enterprise agent continuously monitors agent negotiations, finds out weak links and introduces changes that aim to increase the enterprise value during the process of scheduling.

These interventions are not like a random mutation; they are the result of intelligent problem analysis.

The enterprise agent can offer credit or investments to agents of important clients or of scarce resources to improve their position in the virtual market. Through interventions, the enterprise agent, as the representative of the global schedule, which was constructed by interactions of local agents, influences the performance of these same local agents – an important aspect of self-organisation.

It is important to note that the enterprise agent has no power to order other agents what to do or how to do their jobs; it influences outcomes by adjusting criteria or by triggering agent renegotiation processes, exactly as in modern enterprises, where enlightened executives facilitate rather than instruct.

Constraint Stressing

In transportation logistics there are often constraints that can be easily stressed or even rejected, if no other option can be found.

Consider an example where no truck is allowed to arrive to the warehouse after 1 pm; if, however, a truck according to the schedule is due to arrive at 1.05 pm and if this is the only option that significantly increases the enterprise value, it is worth trying to "stress" this constraint and allow the truck to complete this trip rather than leave the order unallocated.

The decision on constraint stressing may be supported through a review of agent negotiation logs. An agent can be created that is charged to find all rejections given to the order agent of this unallocated order and to sort them by their "closeness" to the acceptance. In this example, 5 minutes may be considered as a relatively small deviation from the rule for the warehouse, and the system may decide to allow constraint stressing autonomously, or to ask the planning operator or warehouse manager for their approval.

In this example the agent log serves as another global structure that is temporally created and exists not only to record decisions but also to find and eliminate weak links in the system. This is a case where the system proposes to the user to review definitions of previous tasks, which were not solved under predetermined constraints.

Balancing Interests of Agents

The schedule quality is considered as a dynamic balance between interests of all independent players in the system under consideration. In transportation logistics such players are clients, orders, transportation instructions, trucks, journeys, driver shifts, cross-docks, etc. All of them have value, goals and preferences and certain amount of virtual money. Note that goals and preferences may change at the individual level during the process of schedule creation by changing the enterprise strategy in response to changing situations. For example, in some situations it is necessary to transport cargoes quicker and cheaper taking into consideration the level of acceptable risk and individual constraints/preferences of cargo owners. In others, it may be required to transport as much cargoes as possible even if it decreases the enterprise profit in order to deliver the expected service level for a VIP customer.

The balance of interests is not the same as equilibrium. Like with all complex adaptive systems, an MAS is never in equilibrium for long (the state where everything is as it should be and there is no motivation for agents to act).

In some cases the balance of interests may be reached only partially, a case when participants in the scheduling process have found an acceptable schedule although some participants are probably still not quite happy with the outcome. The enterprise agent or possibly an operator may intervene in such situations. They can change the weighting between costs, risk, delivery time and service level and thus trigger a new round of local negotiations and a search for new options. The new outcome will have a different "quality" from the business point of view.

In fact at any time the emerging schedule can be considered as a network in an unstable equilibrium, which accounts for high adaptability of multi-agent schedulers.

Communities of Agents

In many cases the speed and effectiveness of agent negotiations can be improved by clustering orders and resources into groups and assigning an agent to act on behalf of all group members. To underline the fact that agents forming a group are still autonomous these groups are called communities of agents. For example, several small orders may not be able to find a place on a big and expensive truck but if consolidated into one big order, they become of interest for carriers and their community agent is put in a position to negotiate a truck, which satisfies requirements of all members of the group.

A community agent may, if it is expedient, temporary make decisions on behalf of the community without any consultation with members expecting that corrections may be necessary when the circumstances allow consultations. For example, if the journey agent decides to change shifts and the shift agent to change trucks, agents unhappy with this decision may leave the new journey at any time and thus "correct" previous decision made without general consultation. Decisions without consultations inevitably improve the speed of the scheduling process and often do not invoke corrections, like in the example where a community agent decides to place a whole community of orders on an unexpectedly available suitable truck and thus increase the enterprise value without needlessly wasting time on prolonged consultations.

It is important to note that the formation or destruction of communities may be initiated autonomously by agents with a view to increasing enterprise value, as discussed in the next chapter.

The type of negotiations taking place at all levels in the virtual world is basically the same, which considerably simplifies the design and coding of the system. Transportation instructions join journey community in the same way as journeys join driver-shift community, or as driver-shift join truck community.

Swarms of Swarms of Agents

A swarm is a group of agents engaged in collective decision-making by negotiation aimed at achieving a specified goal, e.g., producing a dynamic schedule that maximises enterprise value.

If the problem is too large for a swarm to handle, and if the problem can be partitioned in reasonably self-contained sub-problems, then each sub-problem may be assigned to a separate swarm. These swarms are then organised to cooperate/compete with each other. For example, in the road transportation logistics, it is advisable to have separate swarms for loading of trucks, scheduling of trucks, scheduling of drivers and scheduling of truck maintenance and repair.

Costing per Item and per Transaction

MAS designed on the basis of requisite granularity have a considerable advantage because they can provide information on the costing of every single transaction performed on each demand and each resource, provided the values of individual resources and demands as well as unit costs of individual activities applied to the resource (e.g., manufacturing, packaging, storing and transporting a resource) are known. The system is therefore able to calculate the total cost of the whole supply chain per item delivered and per transaction performed (e.g., product A1 cost at delivery = production cost + storage cost + transportation cost).

Adaptive Pricing

Requisite granularity of the model has another advantage in situation in which there is a need to determine the price of a service when information on demand is incomplete, as is the case when an airline sells seats several months in advance of the flight. Agent-based systems can determine the seat price as a function of demand as forecasted, in real time, which changes every time a seat is sold.

Multi-Agent Software as a Complex Adaptive System

To support our claim that multi-agent software is complex, let us demonstrate how our agent-based software satisfies seven criteria of complexity.

Connectivity

Typically, a large number of diverse software agents interact among themselves by exchanging messages. As a rule, connectivity is <1, because not every agent will interact with every other agent. Links between agents can vary in strength and weaker links is much easier to brake in order to establish new ones.

Autonomy

Behaviour of software agents is constrained by scenarios (rules) stored in the knowledge base. Scenarios can be devised to allow agents a certain freedom to autonomously choose which action to undertake, if the knowledge on how to solve the problem at hand is incomplete. For example, agents may be allowed to solve a problem by trial-and-error method.

Emergence

Overall behaviour of MAS is not centrally controlled; it emerges from the interaction of software agents and is unpredictable but not random. As orders arrive and resources are allocated to orders, the strength of links, which are formed between orders and resources, varies depending on the satisfaction with the match. With time, more and more week links get broken and replaced with new stronger links and thus, in time, a schedule emerges from the initial chaos of disconnected objects. In situations in which two equally satisfactory solutions to a problem at hand could be found, it is not possible to predict which one will be selected. However, it is predictable that one will emerge.

Nonequilibrium

MAS are driven by events. The occurrence of a disruptive event triggers activities of affected agents to accommodate the event and if these occurrences are frequent, agents will not have time to accomplish their tasks and rest. Consequently the system will be most of the time in a transient state, far from equilibrium.

Non-linearity

Occasionally the smallest change in external conditions (e.g., the arrival of a new small and insignificant order) causes large changes in the schedule.

The butterfly effect can be controlled by the uneven distribution of virtual money to orders (favouring large orders). To predict such points of bifurcation special "virtual orders" can be used which can play the role of "sensors" forecasting future dramatic changes of schedule.

Under certain conditions, agent negotiations may degenerate into oscillatory behaviour, the condition indicating that the system is at the edge between two attractors and cannot decide which one is more suitable. Oscillations may be amplified as they propagate from node to node in an agent network and may lead to network disintegration unless measures controlling oscillation propagation are implemented (e.g., reducing connectivity or introducing local dampers).

Self-organisation

When a disruptive event occurs in an MAS, an agent is assigned to the event, which will attempt to renegotiate the allocation of resources to demands with affected agents; as a result previously established demand–resource links may be broken and new ones formed autonomously (without external instructions). Weaker links are always broken first, the feature that ensures propensity to improve enterprise value.

Co-Evolution

When MAS is connected to a business process, any change in that process is reflected in the MAS; over a period of time the accumulated changes in the MAS will reflect the accumulated changes in the process. In this way the model co-evolves with the business process.

Comparing Multi-Agent Software with Conventional Programs

Conventional programs allocate resources to demands following pre-programmed algorithms in a sequential manner and therefore, when dealing with a large number of resources and demands, they require a long time to find the optimal allocation. Whenever resources or demands change, these programs start the allocation process from the beginning and if changes are frequent, they oscillate and cannot reach the optimal solution. Centralised intelligent systems are more flexible since they are normally driven by heuristics (rules derived from experience). Nevertheless they still solve the allocation problem in a batch mode and therefore cannot handle frequent changes effectively.

In contrast, complex adaptive software, implemented using ontology and high-granularity multi-agent technology, executes the allocation of resources in non-locking concurrent computations. Typically, hundreds of thousands of agents located on a single server or workstation work concurrently, and if the problem is distributed over many servers and workstations, the number of concurrent allocation processes can rise considerably.

Instead of performing complex computational searches for the best match between demands and resources, agents exchange messages. For example, when a new order arrives the agent assigned to this order will broadcast a call for bids to fulfil the order to all resources; available resources respond and the deal is worked out through negotiations.

This explains how MAS can rapidly arrive at a near-optimal allocation of resources in real time. In cases where changes are infrequent and therefore there is a time between disruptions to rich optimal allocation, agents will systematically reconsider each concluded resource–demand match with a view to increasing the enterprise value. This is a time-consuming process, which agents will carry out in addition to any reallocations due to changes in market conditions. Agents work solving client's problems 24 hours a day and will continue renegotiating partially matched deals until the best possible match is achieved or time runs out.

Agents do not have to wait for instructions. They plan and execute tasks autonomously and are capable of deciding when to compete and when to cooperate with each other. They react to any change in demand or supply without being prompted. Agents representing resources will proactively try to place them by searching for potential customers, offering discounts, cross selling, making special offers and/or cooperating with other agents.

Agents representing people will actively search for resources that match their requirements and will contact their clients, perhaps by sending them emails, when they obtain satisfactory allocations.

MAS can easily be scaled up by organising agents into swarms that cooperate or compete with each other.

Perhaps the most important advantage of agent-based software is that, when a disruptive event occurs, it reschedules only affected parts of the schedule, leaving matches between unaffected demands and resources unchanged. As a result, when an order in a supply chain is cancelled or a resource fails the changes to the overall schedule will be minimal.

4

Emergent intelligence

Fundamentals

Human Intelligence is a complex concept that embraces many features, including:

- Understanding meaning of symbols, words, text, data, images, utterances
- Learning (acquiring knowledge) from data, text, images, from own behaviour, from behaviour of others, as well as by discovery
- Analysing (deconstructing) complicated situations
- Making choices (decisions) under conditions of variety and uncertainty and therefore solving incompletely specified problems and achieving goals under conditions of the occurrence of frequent unpredictable events
- Interacting (communicating) with other actors in the environment, including intelligent creatures and machines
- Autonomously adapting to changes in the environment
- Creating (constructing) new concepts, principles, theories, methods, artefacts, models, literature, music, art
- Setting and achieving goals by competing and/or cooperating with others

An important part of human intelligence is to strive to create artificial intelligence, where "artificial" means man-made rather than natural. Historically artificial intelligence is designed and implemented in computer software and built into artefacts such as robots or intelligent machines [27] appearing in various disguises such as universal problem solvers [28], expert systems [29,30] and neural networks [31].

The authors take a fresh approach to creating artificial intelligence [32]. We assume that

> Artificial intelligence is an emergent property of complex systems.

We test this hypothesis by designing large-scale complex adaptive software, by observing its performance and by studying logs of its behaviour.

It is important to note that the idea is compatible with much of research results in neurophysiology and genetics. A network of several billions of neurons in the human brain is a complex system in which intelligence is not traceable to any individual component (neuron); it emerges from the interaction of these components guided by genetic knowledge built in every cell. Three extraordinary books by Minsky [32] Edelman [33] and Noble [34] were our rich sources of inspiration.

Evidence of Intelligent Behaviour

Let us consider the evidence of intelligent behaviour obtained from observations of performance and from logs of agent interactions in our adaptive road transportation scheduler, the scheduler, for short. These studies show that our software is capable of self-organisation, adaptation, autonomy, achieving goals under conditions of uncertainty, learning and evolution – the behaviour usually associated with intelligence – and since none of their components (agents) are capable of such behaviour in isolation, the only logical conclusion is that intelligence of software is created by the *interaction* of agents; it is an emergent property.

Let us consider some of the most interesting aspect of the scheduler behaviour, *self-organisation, learning, adaptation, achieving goals under conditions of uncertainty and emergence.*

Self-Organisation

As disruptive events occur, agents react by modifying previously agreed demand–resource links to meet new requirements. This rematching represents self-organisation. Agents autonomously (without being instructed) act to achieve their goals pursuing a trial-and-error strategy. We describe in the following sections several examples of self-organisation observed in swarms of agents.

Spontaneous Formation of Communities of Agents

Some situations discovered by studying logs of the scheduler behaviour are quite intriguing, like when several orders that have already been allocated to a truck find the allocation not quite satisfactory and elect to be grouped together and appoint an agent to act as community agent with the task to negotiate their transfer to a smaller truck, a solution that is satisfactory for all members of the group. For illustration, if order 1 needs a transfer of a cargo from A to B, and order 2 from B to C (and the truck then needs to go back to A), the best option is for these two orders to form a group with order 3 from C to A for a backhaul.

Agents of resources with the same or similar attributes and preferences may decide to form a community and start a search for the allocation options for the whole community. If a satisfactory group allocation is not possible, the community agent may ask certain orders to leave the group. Members of the group may be allowed or not to negotiate with their community agent although they can always reply to messages. Individual agents that want to stay in the group may be asked to pay membership fee. Agents who do not approve of work of the community agent can demand dismissal of the community or leave the community to start a search for options by themselves. Communities of agents can form associations that represent more complex hierarchical or networking structures and agents can dynamically create new organisations in order to solve complex problems that they fail to solve individually. In every case communities are formed and disbanded autonomously. We consider this particular aspect of agent organisation as the most significant contribution to the design of agent interaction.

The formation of communities of agents effectively transforms a flat virtual market into a dynamic multi-level structure in which communities may spontaneously spring into existence and after a while may disappear, depending on prevailing conditions. In addition to horizontal agent-to-agent transactions we have now also vertical transactions between community agents and community members, which can be bottom-up, as in the case when an agent decides to leave a community or top-down, as in the case when the community agent asks a member to leave the community.

There is a synergy between the concept of agent community and that of a Holon [35]. Communities, at least temporary, become unique and indivisible entities (Holons) with shared interests, attributes and constraints and common behaviour, performance and achievements. The agent acting on behalf of such a community has similar role as any agent in the virtual world and will address community members only if required, focusing on external to community interactions.

In principle, communities of agents can be considered as organisms characterised by the goal-driven behaviour (seek missing orders), self-organisation (accepting new or expelling existing members to accommodate internally generated requirements for change), protection of boundaries (rejecting unwanted orders or protecting allocations under attack from external agents) and so on.

In addition, each community may organise itself differently to suite its particular needs without ever forming traditional command and control hierarchies, preserving instead the freedom for agents to dynamically belong to several communities and to interact horizontally or vertically depending on prevailing needs.

Spontaneous Acceleration of Negotiations

Another aspect of self-organisation discovered in scheduler logs is equally interesting – spontaneous acceleration of agent negotiations leading to a "constructive destruction" of a schedule in order to create a new schedule of higher quality. Spontaneous acceleration can occur without any apparent cause, akin to autocatalytic processes observed by Nicolis & Prigogine [37].

The acceleration usually leads to the accumulation of virtual money resulting in a kind of explosion or catastrophe (radical changes in the schedule).

Let us consider how this occurs in some detail. A simplified scene of the virtual world is shown in Fig. 15.

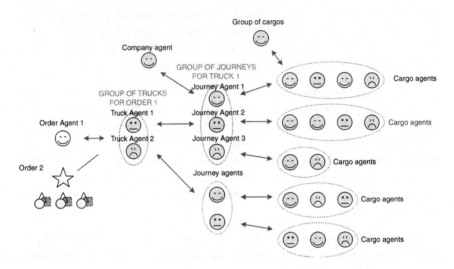

Figure 15: An example of autocatalytic reactions in the scheduler.

The scene depicts a community of several trucks, each in turn containing a community of journeys, each of which containing a community of cargoes. Each link between demands and resources is labelled with two figures denoting the perceived values of the link by both nodes connected by the link.

We can see that the order 1 is satisfied with the allocation of resources. However, some of the resources are for various reasons less satisfied or not satisfied (it may be that the return journeys of some trucks are idle and trucks allocated to some cargoes are inadequate, etc.). However, there is no possibility to improve the current situation and scheduling process is slowing to a standstill. Let us assume that the next event is the arrival of the order 2, which provides for less satisfied and not satisfied agents a new opportunity to improve their allocation. Negotiations will immediately begin between cargoes of order 2 and a suitable truck, which may agree to accept new cargoes and if necessary create new journeys. At the same time, in parallel, many negotiation processes will begin proactively initiated by resources that aim to improve their allocations.

This increased activity of agents sensing new opportunities combined with their dissatisfaction with the decision by the truck agent to accept new cargoes and create new journeys may result in a ripple effect of changes to the schedule, accelerating the rate of change and causing a full collapse of the previously agreed schedule and its immediate rebuilding in a new manner. The schedule thus passes through a slowdown, accelerated activity, collapse into chaos and rebirth, a process known as "constructive destruction".

Behaviour "at the Edge of Chaos"

It is important to note that as the schedule is closer to chaos (i.e., uncertainty is closer to 1), it becomes more sensitive to changes and easier to modify, justifying the expression that the performance of complex systems is the most effective "at the edge of chaos".

Learning

One of the advance features of the scheduler is the ability to recognise regularities, i.e., patterns in data. Such patterns represent knowledge hidden in data. As an illustration, knowledge about the effectiveness of scheduling decisions can be obtained from patterns contained in data on past performances. Similarly, knowledge about markets can be obtained from patterns hidden in data on transportation demands and supplies. Any regularity, i.e., pattern, in the behaviour of a non-deterministic logistic network, reduces the scheduling solution space and can therefore save a considerable effort in searches.

The process of autonomously discovering knowledge from data amounts to learning.

The pattern recognition method used in the scheduler is based on our invention, the adaptive multi-agent clustering [18], where the term cluster denotes a set of similar records (e.g., volume of deposits and age of bank clients or the amount of money that is monthly drawn from the account). Whilst in traditional data mining algorithms the structure of a cluster is rigidly selected for all clusters in advance (e.g., parameters of orders for oil and date of their arrival), in the scheduler, the structure emerges from the clustering process and different cluster can have different structures.

Adaptive clustering can discover completely unexpected patterns in data.

This does not prevent the users to specify their requirements if they know exactly which patterns they are searching for.

The clustering works as follows: an agent is assigned to each record; as soon as created, record agents immediately begin to send messages to each other, searching for similar records with a view to forming clusters; when a number of record agents agree to form a cluster, a cluster agent is created, whose task is to attract further records to the newly created cluster; record agents and cluster agents continue their negotiations until clustering of all record is complete.

Due to the self-organising capability of agent swarms, the process of clustering is very flexible and is usually performed in real time, i.e., whenever a new record arrives the swarm reconsiders previously agreed clusters and decides on the best fit for the new arrival (the process is analogous to that of scheduling in real time, as explained earlier).

Structures of clusters may include sub-clusters (e.g., a cluster of orders "delivery to Europe" may contain several sub-clusters of orders, say, for different types of oil and for different weeks in September). Structures of clusters are likely to change with the arrival of new records, if clustering is done in a dynamic data environment.

Discovery of a cluster implies the existence of rules connecting records that belong to the cluster, and these rules can be used as an empirical generalisation, e.g., orders for certain type of oil come every year from Europe in September. Such rules appear and disappear dynamically and can be used for decision-making only under conditions prevailing during data collection. For example, rules derived from data collected when the logistic environment was distorted due to unforeseen factors such as local armed conflicts at shipping ports or a singular jump in oil prices cannot be used in situations where these factors are absent. Nevertheless, more often than not these rules are very useful discoveries that can be used as forecasts for marketing and sales purposes as well as generalisations for tentative decision-making in scheduling.

Therefore,

> Adaptive systems not only discover patterns in data (learn), they are also capable of autonomously applying acquired knowledge to improve their problem-solving capabilities.

Typical examples of clusters in transportation logistics are orders grouped by their parameters (original location and destination location, geographical areas, volume of delivery, repeating sequence of orders from different customers, shapes of "good" journeys, truck types, etc.). The following pattern "As a rule, long-distance trips are executed by third-party carriers (TPC)", which generates the strategy "We immediately plan long-distance orders to be fulfilled by TPC and only when the schedule is nearly completed we check if it is possible to improve it by assigning own transportation resources". Knowledge about such patterns makes possible to specialise individual agents (e.g., small and close-distance order agents behaves in a different way than big and long-distance order agents). Use of this information in real time allows the users/agents to significantly improve quality and effectiveness of scheduling decisions.

The system is clearly behaving as a complex adaptive system, a swarm, or a team, rather than a computer program. There is no global algorithm to follow (although there are many local ones); there are individual agent goals and guidelines but not step-by-step instructions for the swarm how to achieve the global goals. Each agent pursues its individual goals and as a result of their interaction they collectively achieve global goals – the schedule.

The system is capable of autonomously and rapidly reacting to unpredictable events by rescheduling parts of the overall schedule that were affected by these events. Reactions to the same event at different times are different, depending on the situation at the time of the occurrence of the event. The system usually finds a feasible way of accommodating an event, provided that the solution space exists.

With hindsight any of these actions can be justified given prevailing conditions, but none of them were performed following instructions nor could they have been predicted before they were actually undertaken by the system.

The system autonomously undertakes rather unexpected actions to achieve its goal under conditions of uncertainty created by disruptive events. For example,

- It may find a simple modification that satisfies the new conditions or, to the contrary, it may destroy the previously constructed schedule and rebuild it from scratch.
- It may form and disband increasingly complex communities of agents as powerful global structures which can act autonomously and affect the behaviour of agents.
- Agents may wait for messages and then respond or they may proactively offer their services to other agents.
- Agents may compete with each other or cooperate.
- A spontaneous acceleration of negotiations may occur in horizontal (agent to agent) and vertical (agent to community agent, etc.) interactions, which we consider as a fundamental basis of emergent intelligence.

As we look at the log of agent interaction we see that the solution to every problem emerges step by step. The proposal of the first proactive agent is always improved by reactions to this proposal from other agents. The final decision on the allocation of resources to demands is a result of as many as several hundred *conjectures* and *refutations*, to use Karl Popper's terminology [38].

According to Karl Popper, science advances by a trial-and-error process, as follows. A hypothesis is first proposed which is then tested and results of tests are incorporated into the improved hypothesis, which is again tested. The process is repeated until the hypothesis becomes stable, at which point it could be considered as a new theory. Popper described this process as a sequence of conjectures and refutations. The process is similar to Hegel's dialectics but it proceeds in two rather than three steps: "conjectures and refutations" rather than "thesis, antithesis and synthesis". It is no coincidence that our agent swarms arrive at solutions in exactly the same way: by agent proposals improved by counter-proposals in a stepwise manner until the further improvements are insignificant (diminishing returns) or the system runs out of time.

Emergence

Logs show that our multi-agent software exhibits behaviour that perfectly fits the theory of complex adaptive systems with concepts such as order and chaos, link strength, unstable equilibriums, attractors, bifurcations, catastrophes and nonlinearities. These exceptional aspects of the behaviour of our software, which drastically differ from the deterministic behaviour of purely algorithmic codes, enable it to generate effectively the allocation of resources to demands under volatile dynamic operational conditions with or without interacting with users.

Based on observations of a working large-scale MAS, the scheduler, it is reasonable to arrive at the conclusion that a guided interaction of a large number of relatively simple agents produces behaviour, which for all intents and purposes can be defined as intelligent. We conclude therefore that the critical component of the scheduler described above is its virtual world.

The outstanding research questions are many and include measuring the speed of reactions triggered by events, time required for the schedule to settle down after the ripple, the identification of attractors in the state space of the system and prediction of the conditions under which the system will reach one of the attractors or shift from one to another. The key question is how to guide the interaction of agents, to slow down or accelerate the occurrence of extreme events and trigger the system to reach a desirable attractor.

The uncertainty present in the MAS enables it to create emergent behaviour but also causes some real problems for the system designers, which could be summarised as follows.

- The behaviour of the system is unpredictable in detail although the system always arrives at a balanced solution under circumstances.
- The reaction of the system to events may vary widely from rapid to slow, when a big reconstruction of the schedule is required.
- It is almost impossible to follow cause–effect chains of ripple effects in the presence of a stream of input events.
- The irreversible evolution of the schedule causes problems when attempts are made to roll back.
- The dependence of results on time confuses the analysis of system behaviour.

The results of these investigations will help significantly to achieve better than humans quality and performance of scheduling not only in transportation and all other logistics applications but also in many other complex domains.

Nevertheless the operation of the scheduler at the edge of chaos is so much more effective under conditions of a volatile and highly dynamic global market in comparison with purely algorithmic and rule-based schedulers that it is worth putting up with certain difficulties.

It is revealing to observe an artificial system, designed primarily to produce rather unexciting albeit complex road transportation schedules, behaving similarly to so many important natural and living systems, including social systems and human mind, in which major breakthroughs are achieved by nonlinear reactions at unpredictable moments of time.

Thermodynamics of the Virtual World

Other interesting observations include the analogy between the number of messages arriving at an imagined space unit of a scene per unit time and the temperature of that space unit. Indeed, the greater the density of messages and the larger the number of conflicts that require to be resolved per space unit, the higher is the temperature of this spot and, most likely, the longer it will take to resolve all outstanding issues. Considering that virtual money is equivalent to energy and virtual taxes equivalent to dissipation, and that any equilibrium between demands and supply of resources in a schedule, if reached, will be unstable, we can talk about Prigogine's thermodynamics of the virtual world and use methods analogous to those used in thermodynamics for identifying problematic regions of large schedules with a view to partition them and process them by different swarms on the same or different servers.

PART 2

Commercial applications

We have selected a number of commercial applications, developed by our teams, with a view to demonstrating the power of our method of managing complexity.

Every selected application has been formulated as the allocation of resources to demands and each has a different set of complexity issues that had to be resolved by developing an adaptive scheduler, or semantic processor, or knowledge discovery system.

Some case studies have been slightly modified to protect identity of clients who are shy of publicity.

5

Adaptive scheduling of seagoing tankers

The Problem

Our client was a management company operating one of the largest fleets of Very Large Crude Carrier (VLCC) oil tankers consisting of more than 40 ships and representing just below 10% of world seagoing tanker capacity.

The fleet was used to transport crude oil from Gulf to east and west coasts of the USA and from Columbia to Europe and Asia.

Scheduling of tankers was done by a team of five very experienced and skilled dispatchers. Planning and operations teams managing the fleet, as well as the fleet itself, were spread across many different locations and time zones.

The oil transportation market, in which our client operated, was subject to frequent and unpredictable fluctuations in transportation fees.

There were many other unpredictable factors affecting tanker operation, not least queues of vessels frequently forming in front of the entrance into Panama Canal and fluctuation of fees for passing through the Canal related to the length of queues. Tankers belonging to our client were too big to enter the Canal loaded and therefore they had to unload a part of their cargo, which was then transferred to the other end of the Canal through a pipeline, and reloaded into tanker.

Due to many interdependencies between different components of the schedule small changes in one part of the schedule could have repercussions in another apparently separate part of the schedule, which were difficult to trace.

Resources were highly constrained: vessels had fixed parameters (capacity and types of cargo) that had to be considered when developing a schedule. Moreover, different customers and vessels had different preferences, which had to be taken into account. For example, some vessel owners had blacklists of ports into which their tankers were not allowed to enter, whilst some ports did not allow loading or unloading of vessels, which were not fully insured.

Because of the high cost of scheduling mistakes, the requirement was for schedules to be easy to understand, justify, explain and modify by dispatchers.

The event that prompted the client to think seriously about purchasing a scheduler was a prospect of losing services of their key dispatcher due to sudden illness.

Optimal scheduling was perceived to be a computationally complex (NP-hard) problem and, as a consequence, the use of conventional schedulers was not feasible.

The Solution

Brief Overview

The global oil transportation market in which our client operated was highly complex. It was obvious that the client required an adaptive event-driven multi-agent scheduler, which we developed and commissioned. This was our first major application and the first-ever real-time scheduler for seagoing vessels.

The scheduler consisted of standard elements, as described in Part 1, namely, a knowledge base, virtual world, interfaces and engine, supported by the Java enterprise platform, J2EE. The first version of the scheduler had hardwired ontology, no forecasting and agents that performed in-depth searches.

Knowledge Base

A fragment of ontology for scheduling of tankers is shown in Fig. 16. Classes of objects depicted are tanker, home country, client, owner, order, route, cargo, port of loading, destination port, fuelling location and current state.

Virtual World

Virtual world is populated by the following agents:

Fleet agent (enterprise agent), which is primarily concerned with prioritisation of orders and resources with a view to maximising enterprise value.

Order agent, which searches for the most appropriate resources (vessels, crew) to meet the order, taking into account delivery deadline, cost of the resource (including idle runs and fuelling, etc).

Route agent, which creates the optimal route for tankers considering deadlines, distances, fuelling locations and idle runs.

Tanker agent, which ensures the best possible utilisation of the vessel.

Competitor agent, which monitors pricing of competing fleets and ensures that the client's pricing is competitive.

Cargo agent, which ensures that cargo is loaded into tankers with appropriate attributes considering cargo size, type of oil and transportation fees.

Crew agent, which searches for required crew for tankers considering routing, crew specification, cost per day and tanker schedule.

Port agent, which ensures that only tankers that are cleared for entry into ports are scheduled to enter a port considering mainly political and insurance issues.

Fuelling agent, which searches for the best fuelling locations balancing fuel costs and cost of reaching fuelling locations.

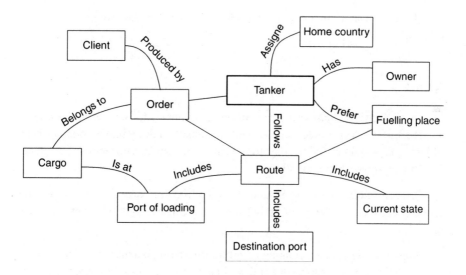

Figure 16: A fragment of tanker ontology.

All allocation decisions are made by negotiation between competent agents. For example, order agents, cargo agents and tanker agents negotiate the allocation of tankers to orders whilst order agents, tanker agents, route agents, port agents and fuelling agents negotiate routes for each tanker.

If a tanker fails and needs repair, the tanker agent send messages to all affected order agents informing them of the disruption. Order agents then renegotiate the allocation of vessels, routes, crew and other resources to meet order requirements.

If fuel price unexpectedly changes at the selected fuelling location, fuelling agent sends messages to affected tanker agents, which in turn renegotiate the routes to switch fuelling to a cheaper location.

Connecting Virtual and Real Worlds

Before our scheduler was implemented the client had in place a centralised database where all information relevant to scheduling was stored and regularly updated. This database was retained as the main repository of information and acted as a communication hub through which our scheduler received and send scheduling messages to the rest of the business.

Each tanker has a terminal directly connected to the scheduling database. Locations of tankers are monitored by GPS and recorded in the scheduling database.

Dispatchers communicate with clients by phone and enter manually their orders and other relevant information into the scheduler database.

Client managers monitored fleet operation via screens connected to our scheduler.

Results

Our first industrial adaptive scheduler achieved commendable savings for the client: a reduction of 3 days of idle runs, per tanker, annually. Taking into account the cost of idle runs per tanker and per day, for 40 tankers the savings generated a return on investment of less than 6 months.

There were other substantial savings more difficult to quantify. Our scheduler reduced significantly delays of oil deliveries and consequently payments of delay penalties.

Domain knowledge on running an oil transportation business was for the first time collected and organised in ontology in a computer readable format and with editing facilities, which enabled easy updating by programmers.

The scheduler was designed to work in autonomous mode or in a decision-support mode.

When in decision-support mode, the requirement was that dispatchers should be provided with feasible scheduling options and cargo delivery price during a telephone conversation with a potential client. That was achieved. The scheduler typically requires few seconds to several minutes to complete the analysis and come up with costing of feasible scheduling options.

6

Adaptive scheduling of taxis

The Problem

At the time when this project was initiated the largest and the best-known minicab (taxi) operator in London had a large fleet of more than 2,000 vehicles, each with a GPS navigation system. The fleet comprised a variety of vehicles, including minivans and SUVs, some with special equipment to match special requirements of clients. At any time around 700 drivers were working concurrently, competing with each other for clients.

The company had a modern ERP system and a call centre with over 100 operators receiving orders concurrently. Some orders were received through the company website. A large team of skilled dispatchers allocated vehicles to customers.

Main characteristics of the taxi service were as follows:

- A very large number of orders: more than 13,000 orders per day.
- The order flow occasionally exceeded the rate of 1,500 orders per hour
- Order arrival times and locations were unpredictable.
- A large variety of clients, e.g., personal, corporate, VIPs, with a variety of discounted tariffs and with special requirements such as suitable for disabled, with a child seat and suitable for transportation of pets.
- A large number of freelance drivers who leased cars from the company and were allowed to start and finish their shifts at times that suited them, which may have differed from one day to another.
- Guaranteed pickup of clients in central London was within 15 minutes from the time of placing the order.
- The requirement was to find the best economic match of vehicles to every clients.
- Exceptions to this requirement, which could change at any time, included matching drivers that drive home after finishing their shifts with passengers travelling in the same direction (to reduce drivers' idle runs) and giving priority to drivers that during a particular day had less work than others (to increase drivers' satisfaction with working conditions).

Events that triggered scheduling and rescheduling included:

- The arrival of new orders
- Changes or cancellations of orders
- Changes in driver profiles
- Changes in driver status or location
- No-shows of clients
- Failures of vehicles
- Delays due to traffic congestion
- Delays due to queues at airports and railway stations.

Scheduling of vehicles and drivers under such conditions represented an exceedingly complex task, which was not feasible to achieve with any known mathematical method.

The Solution

Brief Overview

The source of complexity for a taxi business is high unpredictability and high variety of locations of demand, volatile urban traffic conditions, very high frequency of disruptive events and diversity of driver preferences.

Our solution was an adaptive MAS capable of rapidly, within few seconds, rescheduling the allocation of taxis to customers, to accommodate any disruptive event [39].

Briefly, the schedule was constructed by negotiation between the order agent and driver agents representing drivers that are within reach of the customer. As the demand for taxis and availability of vehicle changed, the system reacted to every change by reallocating drivers to customers, in real time, making sure that the proposed change of the schedule improved the enterprise value.

The scheduler acted as a "virtual client" for the company operational platform. It functioned on a client computer getting all information required for decision-making and for autonomous allocation of resources through an application server.

The system functions 24 hours a day and consists of several modules inter-connected by the event queue. It works in several threads and changes system configuration when required. For example, for testing purposes, the system may use loaders of XML scenarios or historical data.

Knowledge Base

Ontology nodes are classes of objects involved in taxi business, which include customer, order, vehicle and driver.

Order attributes are:

- Location of pickup and drop
- Pickup urgent or booked in advance (for a certain date and time)
- Type of service (standard car, minivan, VIP, etc.)
- Importance of service (a number from 0 to 100 depending upon the client)
- Special requirements (pet, child chair, etc.)

Driver/vehicle attributes are:

- Type of vehicle
- Capability to complete special jobs
- Driver experience (novice or experienced)
- Location where drivers lived
- Current vehicle location (GPS coordinates)
- Driver status ("unavailable", "break", "working", "free", "will be free in 5/10 minutes", "goes home")

Factual data on resources and demands (object instances) are stored in relational databases.

Scenes depict instantaneous models of the taxi business giving locations of all vehicles, their availability, etc.

Virtual World

The allocation of taxis to customers is done by the negotiation between order agents, assigned to customers and driver agents, assigned to taxi drivers. Order agents are active: they compile lists of available vehicles and initiate negotiations with driver agents. Driver agents, in the first version of the system, were designed to be only reactive: they only replied to requests from order agents and implemented the selected option. In general, order agents and driver agents compete with each other or cooperate, depending on what is best for the whole enterprise. In this particular solution we have used, in addition to order and driver agents, some new types of agents, namely external events agents, regional loading agents and orders allocation agent.

Agents were designed to use flexible decision-making criteria instead of direct priorities, which is valuable when there is a need to deal with different categories of clients. For example, if a VIP order arrives and there is only one cab that fully corresponds to the specified requirements and if that cab is already assigned to another job, the system will nevertheless allocate the VIP order to this vehicle and initiate rescheduling of the previously agreed matches, if required.

The system first attempts to maximize company profit. Then, other criteria that are important for the business are considered, such as the service level. Also, when choosing from two approximately equal options the system sends the order to that driver who did not receive orders for a long time, thus ensuring relatively fair distribution of orders.

Agent-based scheduling system was designed to work effectively with human dispatchers. In a situation where one dispatcher takes new order and schedules a vehicle to come from north to south to pick up a client, and another dispatcher independently schedules another vehicle to go from south to north for another order, the agents can spot this anomaly in the schedule and recommend to dispatchers to change their decisions.

The taxi allocation system functions in short cycles. Between the cycles the system collects the events and places them in a queue. In each cycle, the events from the queue are processed, one by one, and appropriate agents are, in turn, given control by the system dispatcher. Each event initiates a chain of negotiations between agents. When all events are processed and the system is satisfied that the best possible schedule is produced, the system falls asleep until a new event arrives. Options are evaluated using the cyclic transfer algorithm.

To decrease the dimensions of the decision space, a pre-matching mechanism was used, which determines the suitability of matching of orders to drivers. This mechanism cuts off unpromising options.

Microeconomics was used to evaluate and compare the order–driver pairs that were created at the previous step. An evaluation mark is given to each option and good options are remembered so that the evaluations do not need to be repeated later. The evaluation mark is determined using multi-criteria model and calculated as a sum of all criteria values multiplied by their weights.

The following criteria were used for option evaluation: distance to the order, predicted delay of the pickup, if any, preferences of the driver (priority given to the drivers that did not have orders for a long time), driver experience, distance of the driver to overloaded area (to utilize drivers from outlying districts), service level conformity, importance and priority of the order, driver's place in a queue (if he is waiting at an airport), driver's home address (if he is looking for an order on the way home).

Scheduling workflow included the following steps:

1. New order comes to the event queue.

2. Possibility of order scheduling is checked.

3. The order receives an agent.

4. All drivers that can complete this order are included in pre-matching (to cut off unpromising options).

5. Evaluation of all driver–order pairs is done according to criteria based on microeconomics.

6. The order agent requests order completion costs from selected driver agents. This cost includes the cost of transferring the order from the previously allocated driver.

7. The driver receives the information on the reallocation costs by sending a request to its current order.

8. If the revised decision is better than the previous one, it is applied.

9. Process described in step 6 continues for all candidate drivers, for whom the initial evaluation (without transfers) was better than the current evaluation.

10. If no changes occur during the cycle, the event processing is considered finished.

In order to achieve a solution as near as possible to the optimum, the system introduces a delay between the allocation of a taxi to a client and the point in time at which it sends pickup instructions to the driver (commitment). During this time interval the vehicle is considered to be available for new allocations, but any new allocation is effected only if the proposal leads to the improvements of performance indicators. When required, driver agents attempt "to come to an agreement" with each other about proposed reallocation of orders, occasionally offering a compensation to the driver that looses a good client in order to improve overall value of the business. Very often the rescheduling of allocated resources leads to a wave of negotiations aimed at the resolution of conflicts between new and old orders. The length of the rescheduling chain is limited only by the time required to reach a client in the busy city such as London, which normally is sufficient for several changes of the schedule. Thus, the system builds a schedule and perpetually reviews it, as long as there is a possibility to improve KPIs, and the time for essential rescheduling is still available.

For each order the commitment time is dynamically calculated taking into account the priority and service type of the order and some other parameters. When commitment time expires, information about the order is sent to a driver and the order is removed from the scheduler. The introduction of the dynamic commitment time resulted in the increase of the fleet effectiveness by reducing the average task completion time per driver.

When new order arrives the system automatically finds the best vehicle and makes a preliminary booking. On average, it takes 9 minutes to provide a vehicle for an urgent order. Orders with specified time of pickup are immediately allocated, but the system continues reallocating these orders as new suitable vehicles become available and does not commit the final decision until the point in time when the driver must start a journey to complete the order. During the interval between the arrival of an urgent order and commitment time, the system usually improves the initial allocation of drivers to the customer several times.

If drivers were allowed to act purely according to personal preferences, a surplus of drivers would occur in some regions and insufficient numbers in others. To prevent such situations an option was introduced to distribute the fleet according to the order flow forecasts. Having information about the current order flow and distribution of orders in the past, the expected order flow is extrapolated, enabling the system to generate short-term (30 minutes) forecasts, which are normally reasonably correct. Based on the forecast, the system sends to unoccupied drivers text messages with recommendations to stay in or move to the region where an increased order flow is expected. This feature enables an improved distribution of the fleet, reducing response times and idle miles and increasing the number of pickups. If there is a probability that a VIP order may arrive at a distance from the point where drivers were advised to congregate, the system may recommend to a driver to move closer to the likely order point, offering him in return a guaranteed next order. This is an important feature because productivity of work in overloaded areas determines the actual fleet effectiveness – in areas that are not overloaded there are usually enough drivers to complete available orders. This functionality was supported by a pattern recognition algorithm that can forecast the location of the next order using agent-based dynamic data mining.

In the normal mode of scheduling, drivers who are directed to overloaded areas may be intercepted by newly arrived orders. For example, a driver who drives towards the centre of the city, where there are many outstanding orders, and who is still at a point where these orders are out of his visibility area (the maximum distance where orders allocation is allowed) may be allocated another order, which is within his visibility area, even if it is not as urgent as one in the city centre. As a result, some drivers may never get to the problematic area. To remove this anomaly, the system may temporary amend criteria for the allocation and thus enable drivers to reach critical locations without being intercepted. This is done by raising a flag in the operational platform to indicate that drivers are temporarily restricted to accepting only urgent orders in the critical area even from clients with a low priority. When appropriate, the system may temporarily extend the area where drivers are allowed to search for orders. As soon as the loading distribution improves, the limitations are annulled.

The system tries to identify drivers' attempts to cheat. Since all interactions of the system with drivers are automated, from time to time, drivers attempt to gain personal advantages by giving deliberately false information. The following cases have been recorded:

- Drivers attempt to reduce waiting time by reporting that they are waiting in an airport queue when, in reality, they may be tens of miles far from the airport.
- Drivers attempt to get an earlier order by pressing key "free in 10 minutes" although they may be at the beginning of their assignment.
- Drivers attempt to receive orders in a particular direction several times during a day by pressing key "goes home" several times.

To reduce cheating driver agents monitor driver schedules and, when appropriate, ignore their requests.

During the system implementation other changes aimed at improving the effectiveness of the scheduling process were introduced, e.g., a mechanism for the allocation of orders, which are preliminary booked by drivers, to be completed on the way from home on the next day.

Minimising consequences of disruptions are assured by following the procedure described in the next section. When a disruptive event (e.g., arrival of a new order for a taxi or a change of a driver's status) occurs, only affected agents are engaged in negotiation how to react to the event and only affected parts of the schedule are modified.

Connecting Virtual and Real Worlds

The system communicates with customers and drivers. Customers ring the call centre or visit the website to order, modify or cancel a vehicle and information is entered into the system. Drivers communicate with the system using GPS, mobile phones or specialised hand-held devices, conveying information on their location, direction of travel and availability and receiving instructions to pick up customers.

Results

The system began its operation and maintenance phase in March 2008, only 6 months from the beginning of the project.

Results were extremely good: 98.5% of all orders were allocated automatically without dispatcher's assistance; the number of lost orders was reduced by up to 2%; the number of vehicles idle runs was reduced by 22.5%. Each vehicle was able to complete two additional orders per week spending the same time and consuming the same amount of fuel, which increased the yield of each vehicle by 5–7%.

Time required to repay investments was 2 months from the beginning of the operational and maintenance phase. During the first month of operation the fleet utilization effectiveness was increased by 5–7%, which, in absolute numbers, gives the same fleet an opportunity to complete additional orders bringing 5 million dollars per year. The additional income is being distributed between company and drivers. According to available statistics, since 2008 driver wages have increased by 9%, and there is a possibility for an overall fleet growth.

Further improvements include a reduction of delayed pickups by 3 times, which brought a considerable improvement of service levels for the customers. Urgent order average response time (from booking till arrival for pickup) is now 9 minutes, which is the best time in London. For high priority orders the response time is not greater than 5–7 minutes. A reduction in response time is especially noticeable in overloaded areas.

Search for orders on the way home and improved allocation mechanism, when compared with a previous system, gives 3,000–4,000 miles reduction in daily fleet run, which is of benefit to both drivers and city ecology.

Further developments may include an analysis of vehicle movements to determine actual speed of vehicles, a partial optimisation of the business taking into account courier deliveries (the basic advantage of courier service is having several orders per one courier) as well as other changes targeting the improvements of business effectiveness.

A Russian TV news programme referenced this project and, as a result, the taxi company became a finalist of The Orange Best Use of Technology in Business Award 2008.

7

Adaptive scheduling of car rentals

The Problem

Our client was one of the largest car rental companies in the world and the brief was to develop a real-time scheduler for the UK operation and to expand it, at a later stage, across Europe.

The territory, which we initially covered was partitioned into several regions each with a number of rental stations, where orders for rental were arriving, cars were parked and serviced and drivers begun their working day. At each station there were experienced dispatchers engaged in manual scheduling of drivers and cars. Dispatchers cooperated with both clients and drivers, flexibly correcting schedules if required. Considering a big picture and optimising the overall enterprise operation was beyond their remit, but also beyond their skills and capabilities.

The problem involved making a number of interlinked decisions:

- From which station to take the car, considering preferences of the client, distances, costs and availability of cars at stations.
- Which driver to ask to wash and deliver the car in accordance with the business processes of the company.
- Which driver (runner) to ask to deliver and collect the driver to the car location.
- How to minimise driver overtime.
- How to deliver assigned driver to the chosen car.
- Where and how to return the driver (back to original station, to another rental or to home); very often for this purpose another car and another driver are required and then the complexity increases to a level that cannot be resolved manually nor by conventional planning software.

Frequently occurring disruptive events included new unexpected demands for rentals; previously received demands cancelled or modified; cars breakdown; drivers become ill or take day off; driver arrive late; drivers cannot find the client of the delivered car, or keys of the car that need to be collected; drivers misplace their mobile phones.

Major criteria for making scheduling decisions were car/driver run cost per mile, the penalty for late delivery to rental, the penalty for late delivery of the returned car, cost of drivers' overtimes and the penalty for rental upgrade/downgrade.

The car rental operation is characterised by frequent conflicts between orders. Here are some examples:

- In general it is important that cars are returned to station as soon as possible and delivered, as late as possible, but in case of a large number of rentals and practical impossibility to carry out all tasks in time, the priority must be given to delivery of the most urgent reservations.
- The system should plan working hours of drivers effectively but should balance them with optimising deliveries. For example, if it is necessary to make delivery of a car to a station tomorrow then it is not economically viable to send a driver there today to collect a different car, even if this driver is free; a consolidated trip tomorrow is more effective.
- If there are serious delays it is better to postpone a cheap collection of a car and to execute new delivery in time.
- In general, in order to reduce unnecessary movement of cars, the collection of cars should be done only if there is a demand for them elsewhere; however, if there is a probability that the demand may be created in the near future, the collection may be necessary to reduce risk of interrupting rental flow.

Combining planning and execution is the key requirement for schedulers for rent-a-car businesses. The system is required not only to generate and update schedules but also to provide instruction for the execution of planned tasks and to monitor their fulfilment. Instructions for the execution of scheduled tasks are sent to mobile devices of managers and drivers who are expected to confirm the beginning and the end of each operation, because the delay of one operation can cause a chain of re-planning for others.

It is expected from the system to schedule 100% of all reservations as specified in rental agreements, to strictly meet constraints of drivers' rota, to deliver drivers to home stations at the end of the day, never to leave drivers in the field without a car, and to comply with the planned sequence of tasks during the preparation and delivery of a car. The number of options for each decision in this process is very large and the frequency of occurrence of disruptive events is high.

Designing a scheduler that can cope with such a variety of operating conditions, handle uncertainty related to the occurrence of events and at the same time continuously produce schedules that maximise the set of specified criteria are real intellectual challenges. To the best of our knowledge such schedulers have not been proposed in the literature or implemented in practice.

The Solution

Brief Overview

Complexity of a business of renting cars is quite different from that of running taxis. The key problem here is the long sequence of interdependent activities of drivers, as they pursue appropriate business processes, and a large number of different locations for renting and sourcing cars and drivers, rather than the high frequency of events. It is very difficult to be sure that you have answered cost-effectively questions such as Where to source the type of the car requested for renting? Where to park a returned car? Where to source a driver or a runner?

Our solution was a multi-agent scheduler capable of coordinating many inter-related agent negotiations [40]. Agents are assigned to all demands, as soon as they arrive to the system, and they compete for available resources by negotiating the allocation with resource agents: Rental agent negotiates with car agents to obtain desired car; delivery agent negotiates with driver agents to obtain a driver to deliver the car to the rental location; driver agent negotiates with other driver agents to find "runners" who will deliver the driver to the rental location and collect him/her after the completion of the job, etc. As situation changes, i.e., as new rental orders arrive, previously placed orders are changed, deliveries of cars to locations are delayed, drivers get ill, etc., agents renegotiate the schedule to accommodate these events in real time. All negotiations aim to increase enterprise value.

Knowledge Base

Conceptual knowledge of the rent-a-car domain is stored in ontology as a network whose nodes are classes of objects (concepts) and links are their relations. Ontology is partitioned into three parts (sub-ontologies):

Part 1 includes rent-a-car business object classes, like reservation, car, driver and client.

Part 2 includes scheduling object classes, like task, option and operation. Logical sequences of tasks and operations are specified in this part.

Part 3 includes object classes defining the virtual world of agents, like decision criterion, bonus and penalty (e.g., for late collection, early delivery, driver overtime, late reservation, leaving a driver in the field without a car). Users can directly influence agent decision processes by specifying values for instances of these concepts.

Ontology was designed for easy editing by the client to accommodate changes in the client's business (Fig. 17).

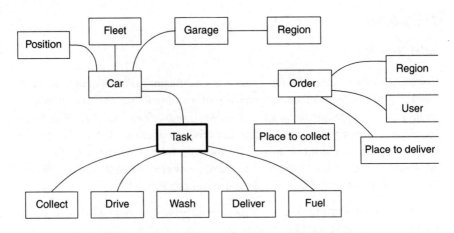

Figure 17: A fragment of rent-a-car ontology.

A typical scene depicts which car is reserved for a particular rental and which driver is driving which car, etc. Scenes represent interdependencies in the given problem situation allowing agents to track easily all important links between objects, operations and participants (Fig. 18).

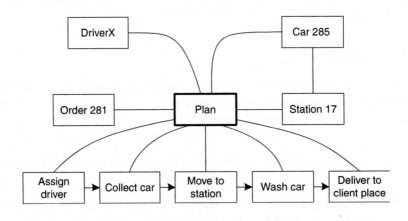

Figure 18: Example of a rent-a-car scene.

Virtual World

The allocation problem is solved by dynamic interaction of agents representing demands and resources. Key agent types are rental agent, client agent, order agent, station agent, car agent, driver agent, delivery agent, collection agent, and wash task agent.

The scheduling process starts by dividing a composite task "to deliver a car" into several constituent sub-tasks. Every sub-task initiates a complex mechanism of agent negotiations. For example, station agent searches for the car and creates the subordinated wash task agent, which searches for the driver most suitable to wash delivered car in time. In more complex cases the quantity of sub-tasks can be quite large, and tasks can establish the interdependences. For example, rental agent searches for the best car, the car agent in turn searches for the best driver and the driver agent searches for another driver (runner) to return the first driver back home after car delivery. Searches are done through the exchange of messages among agents rather than using search algorithms.

Negotiation between agents aimed at allocating the most suitable resources to tasks often discovers conflicts, which have to be resolved. For example, if the only suitable car available to a rental agent is already reserved by another client, the conflict may be resolved by adjusting allocation parameters to suit both clients, or by partial rescheduling, whichever gives the best overall solution.

The links between demands and resources established during interaction of agents are not permanent. On the contrary, as long as there is still time before the commitment point, agents continue to search for improvements to the agreed schedule and may break old links and create new ones. Every agent has propensity to improve the allocation process and may initiate the improvement (agent proactivity).

For example, if for any reasons, the chosen driver is not available any more (human error, accident, etc.) his/her agent will be activated to find all rentals that will be affected and to inform them of the unavailability of the previously allocated resource. Agents of these rentals are then activated to search for suitable resources and to restart negotiations, which may result in partial rescheduling of the operation.

Interactions of agents are shown in Fig. 19, where the main agent classes and relations between them are presented.

In this architecture, every task and sub-task have their own agents, which are called demand agents. Their main goal is to attract the most suitable resources, the activity that may involve a prolonged negotiation if any of resource agents refuse to accept their offers. Agents of different task and sub-task types may have different decision-making logic. Demand agents may need to inform other agents about results of their activities.

The main role of resource agents is to respond to offers from demand agents, which they base on estimates of the costs of the allocation of resources to tasks (rentals). Every resource agent is capable of calculating preliminary cost (average cost) as well as the full cost of matching of the resource to a rental (marginal cost) and to break the initial task into some smaller tasks. The most important function of a resource agent is to create "promise" (obligation) to carry out a task given to the resource for the specified sum.

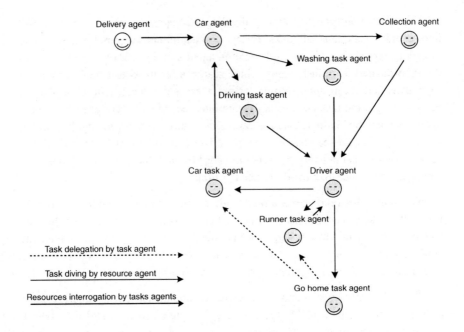

Figure 19: Agent interaction.

The rent-a-car multi-agent scheduler operates with seven types of demand agents, each corresponding to a type of task: delivery, washing, driving, collecting, running, car and go home. It also has two types of resource agents: car, driver.

The majority of allocations are initiated by demand agents (scheduling and rescheduling of a new reservation, change of details of car collection, etc.). But in some cases resource agents are given an active role. They can send messages to demand agents searching for a task for which the given resource would be the best option and, if successful in locating such a task, they would initiate rescheduling.

In cases when a disruptive event renders a previously allocated task or a resource non-available, the agent of this task/resource will initiate rescheduling.

The event-driven, stepwise allocation process does not guarantee construction of the optimum schedule, for all resources and for each moment of time. Therefore, if the time before commitment allows, various methods are used to improve the schedule, in a "trial-and-error" mode.

This includes the use of approximations, average indicators of price values and various heuristics. In addition, we have introduced the enterprise agent, which reviews schedules from time to time and reports on inefficient use of resources, if any. Using this information preselected agents attempt to renegotiate their deals. Also, proactivity cycles of resource agents are introduced, as described above.

Occasionally agents may decide to destroy the schedule and start scheduling from the beginning ("constructive distraction" is the term for such activity).

Any proposed modification of the schedule is accepted only if it results in an improvement in KPIs for the whole systems. Here is an example. If the driver is in the field after a car delivery when he is given a new task and is waiting for a long time for the allocated runner, it is very likely that during this period a different runner will arrive to collect a different car, in which case the system will change the schedule and assign the newly arriving runner to pick up the waiting driver.

The multi-agent scheduler never stops working. It is always monitoring changes in its environment and attempting to improve the schedule.

Connecting Virtual and Real Worlds

The system communicates with customers and drivers. Customers ring the call centre or visit the website to order, modify or cancel a car and information is entered into the system. Drivers communicate with the system using GPS, mobile phones or specialised hand-held devices, conveying information on their location, the beginning and end of each task (delivering or returning a car, washing a car, delivering or collecting a driver, etc.) and receiving instructions to undertake the next task.

Architecture

The core of the solution is a network of multi-agent schedulers each dedicated to a region (one region can contain a number of stations). Regional schedulers allocate resources for all stations in their region.

Each scheduler allocates cars to rentals, issues instructions for drivers to deliver/collect/wash cars, pick up other drivers or transport drivers to collection points. Schedulers work in real time promptly modifying schedules whenever a disruptive event, such a change of reservation, occurs.

In the first version of our solution all regional schedulers are working independently. It is envisaged for them to interact and coordinate their decisions, scheduling cars across regional boundaries and sharing driver resources.

Operational Data Source (ODS) is a read-only storage of operational information about cars, rentals, reservations, rate codes, non-revs, car models and stations. It is a mediator between existing fleet and rental management system and multi-agent schedulers.

Multi-agent scheduler database is a relational database which stores operational information (rentals, car schedules, driver schedules, etc.) and reference data (cars, makes, models, rate codes, stations, journey times, etc.). It is integrated with the internal data backbone to provide read/write access to data about other components.

Offline Archive is a simple file storage in a folder on the logical disk. Data can be retrieved from it manually using any file manager.

Operational data from scheduler database older than a defined time interval (e.g., 2 week) is regularly automatically archived to limit the size of the database and ensure stable performance of read/write operations.

Data backbone is an internal component, which provides a simplified read/write access to the data stored in permanent storage (scheduler database). It is integrated with all components: archiving, workflow support, JTM, pre-processing and scheduling engine.

The system is integrated with a mobility solution, which enables wireless communication with drivers at stations or in field. It is integrated with workflow support component to issue instructions to drivers and get confirmations of completion, ETA updates, information on failed tasks, etc.

Workflow support component is used by scheduling engine to issue instructions to drivers. It delivers confirmations and information about exceptions back to scheduling engine.

Routing software provides time estimation for travelling between two specific postcodes (postcodes sectors) for JTM component. It also provides visual representation of routes (optional).

JTM provides driving time estimation info to scheduling engine and caches information from routing software to ensure acceptable performance.

Pre-processing component exports information from ODS to scheduler database. It checks consistency of data against various rules and raises tasks for the user to validate automatic decisions (e.g., re-rents) or correct data (like missing or incorrect postcode);

System administrator can modify scheduling engine settings to adjust the scheduling logic.

User Interfaces

The system provides a comprehensive desktop user interface for day-to-day station activities (tasks, operational information about cars, drivers and their schedule), fleet managers (fleet movements functionality) and administrator (except management and system maintenance). Client application is automatically deployed and updated on user PC via Java Web Start service.

The tasks screen for station users opens by default when a station user enters the system.

The driver screen displays all drivers and their working hours planned for the current week by weekdays and the total number of hours. To see tasks currently planned for a driver user selects driver in the list. Tasks are listed in the chronological order.

Settings allow system administrator to adjust the criteria, which define the scheduling logic.

Results

The first version of the system was tested on a network of stations of one of the subsidiary of our rent-a-car client with 250 cars and 30 drivers. The business handles 15–20 reservations per day per station and the average frequency of disruptive events is 80–120 per hour. Events include arrivals of new orders and inputs from hand-held devices of drivers and from users.

The scheduler required from 15 milliseconds to 130 seconds to process an event, each event triggering the scheduling of 150–200 tasks. Drop rate (the number of tasks cancelled by the task that survived to commit) was 5–15, depending on the time available for negotiations.

The number of simultaneously active agents was task agents – 2,500, car agents – 250 and driver agents – 30.

The number of options per decision was 5–50, depending on the time of the day and the depth of negotiations was limited to 10.

The importance of real-time scheduling and of delayed commitment is underlined by the following statistics: 40% of disruptive events required substantial rescheduling and 90% of all executed decisions were made 20–30 minutes before the commitment time, whilst only 1% of decisions were made more than 1 hour before the commitment time.

The proactivity of resource agents helped to rapidly (within 2–3 minutes) improve the quality of the schedule, which was drastically reduced every time when urgent disruptive events occurred.

8

Adaptive scheduling of road transport

The Problem

The scheduling requirements of the road transportation industry are very complex. The complexity is caused by:

- Many possible solutions (a very large solution space), which rules out traditional combinatorial search algorithms.
- A very high variety and quantity of transportation demands and resources, which makes formulation of an optimisation function extremely difficult.
- Uncertainty due to high dynamics and volatility of the operational environment, which makes optimisation impractical – a single optimisation run is typically an order of magnitude longer than a typical interval between two consecutive changes in operational conditions.

Let us consider the road transportation scheduling complexity in some detail. The scheduler is required to:

- Handle transportation instructions (TI) from many different loading points to many different destinations (e.g., customer locations and cross-docks, where cargoes are offloaded and consolidated).
- Consider many different routes by which orders can be delivered (routing problem).
- Allocate cargoes of many different sizes and weights to many different types of trucks with or without different types of trailers.
- Take into account preferences of owners, operators and drivers.
- Fit the schedule into numerous constraints imposed by warehouse working hours, driver work rules, safety regulations and enterprise policies, e.g., on choosing between own fleet and third-party carriers.
- Take into account that different logistics companies participating in the supply chain have different critical constraints and different criteria for allowing the scheduler to override certain constraints to achieve a more effective schedule.
- Ensure that the schedule offers opportunities for backhauls and consolidations.

- Accommodate the frequency and variety of unpredictable disruptive events such as the arrival of new unexpected orders, cancellations, failures, bad weather conditions, road works and no-show of drivers or loading crews.

To enable enterprises to plan and re-plan continuously, reacting to events in real time, scheduling is divided into "Planning/Commit/eXecute" (PCX) stages and reaches across a multi-day planning horizon.

In the planning stage orders are assigned to trucks and truck journeys are constructed. During this stage orders can be added or removed and the route planned for a truck can be changed as a result of subsequent events.

At some point there is a need to commit the truck. This will trigger communications to warehouses, driver shift planners, truck servicing, etc., to make ready the truck for its journey. During this phase changes to the truck schedule are undesirable because there would be knock-on effects for the warehouse, driver assignment, etc.

The execute stage starts with the driver performing his pre-journey checks and continues until his debriefing at the end of his shift is completed. During this phase a high level of sophistication is needed to alter the truck schedule in transit.

To achieve competitive advantage it is necessary to consider real-time conditions and make the allocation decisions taking into account detailed analysis of the current situation, rather than following rigid rules. By calculating the profitability of each order, truck and journey, using a dynamic cost model, it is possible to produce a realistic "the best possible under circumstances" schedule rather than an unrealistic "optimal" schedule. For example, a standard rule-based scheduler would not allow a nearly empty truck to start a journey whilst a truck loaded by only 10% of its capacity may be very profitable if it is loaded with a special cargo.

The Solution

Brief Overview

A road transportation problem has unique salient features: relatively long period of time between the commitment point and the beginning of a journey during which new orders cannot be allocated to trucks; a very high diversity of cargoes that have to be transported from a high diversity of locations to a high diversity of destinations within a high diversity of deadlines; and a high cost of idle return journeys, which have to be avoided.

Our solution is a rather large multi-agent scheduler designed to coordinate many interdependent agent negotiations and to allocate resources initially based upon the dynamic forecasting of the arrival of orders. The scheduler continuously modifies the initial schedule to accommodate disruptive events, in real time and, whenever possible, improves the initial allocation, with a view to increasing enterprise value [41,47].

Formalised knowledge is in ontology supported by a powerful ontology editor. Agents negotiate scheduling decisions in the virtual world, which is occasionally referred to as virtual market because it supports "trading" between agents.

The scheduler is implemented on a J2EE platform.

The main window of the scheduler allows importing orders and placing them in the queue, starting planning and reviewing the schedule using a Gantt chart and map, including detailed information about journeys and key performance indicators. Different parts of the window can be easily configured and rearranged. At any moment users can view an agent inspector showing which agents are currently working in the system. To check how agents made allocation decisions users can analyse the agent negotiation log.

Knowledge Base

Object classes stored in ontology were order, TI, cargo, truck, journey, etc. linked by relations such as "journey consists of TI".

Ontology was divided into three main parts, as shown in Fig. 20.

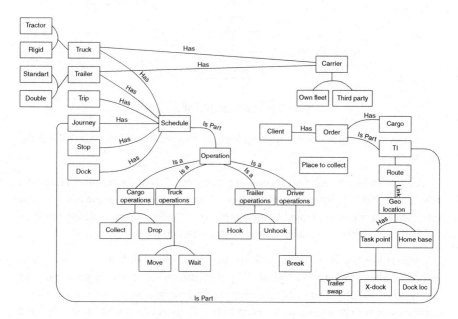

Figure 20: Typical road transport ontology.

1. Basic ontology included main logistics concepts such as client, carrier and fleet

2. Scheduling ontology included resources such as truck, trailer, trip, journey and schedule, and contained references to the operations, which constitute schedules, described in operation ontology.

3. Operations ontology included operation performed upon resources such as collect, move, drop and hook.

This structure allows the introduction of new types of operations into schedules at any time.

A typical scene is shown in Fig. 21. The scene representation is designed to help the user to understand the network state at any time. For example, looking at "client" it is possible to find out where all TIs are at any given moment and looking at "location" it is possible to see all journeys that are planned to go through this location.

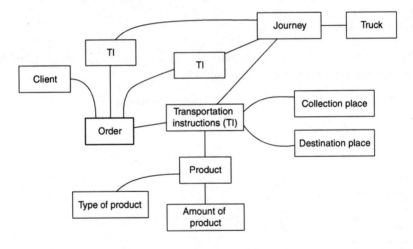

Figure 21: An example of a scene.

Scenes also make decision-making logic more visual and understandable to the end-users.

Conceptual knowledge on scheduling is separated from the resource allocation mechanism, which greatly simplifies updates and increases the reuse of code. The process of formalising domain knowledge helps in refining it and closing the gaps left due to the empirical nature of knowledge collection.

Scenes are the basis for a sophisticated interaction with users. The user is informed about the current situation by the current scene and is given support for decision-making. The fact that a scene is a formalised description of a business situation helps to recognise patterns and identify gaps in the user knowledge and understanding.

Virtual World

The scheduler has several key types of agents, including:

Customer agent – looks after the required customer service level.

Order agent – splits orders into TIs and monitors order KPIs. Finds TIs whose allocation is unsatisfactory and tries to improve their situation by searching for the best journey.

TI agent – searches for the best journeys.

Journey agent – looks for the best TI, devises good consolidation, looks for the best routes with minimal mileage.

Cross-dock agent – supports the schedule for cross-docks and allocates journeys into time slots.

Group agent – keeps similar TIs together.

Enterprise agent – minimises fixed costs by decreasing number of trucks used; switches company strategies; monitors schedules and causes disturbances to destroy "bad" journeys.

Each type can act as a demand agent or a resource agent depending on the situation. Demand and resource are the roles that agents can play.

The scheduler has a generic virtual world architecture, which enables agents to form natural coalitions, e.g., TIs on a journey or journeys, which together constitute a driver shift (all journeys made by a driver during his working day). This means that virtual world is multi-level, as shown in Fig. 22, with nested groups formed by common interests where each group has an agent representative (group agent) who monitors what is happening in the group. Agents can join the group and leave it. The whole group can move (e.g., journey goes to another driver shift).

This architecture provides flexibility in developing communities of different types of agents, which can work as coalitions. Such approach also gives more options to find right balance between interests of individual egoistic agents (TI, journey, etc.) and interests of communities of agents (fleet, journey, etc.). Also, the balance can be changed dynamically, reacting to events (e.g., X-Dock under terrorist attack).

Finally, this architecture forms the basis for ongoing self-improvement of schedules. The generic architecture provides stable, well-designed and elegant basis for rapid development of new applications in a wide range of new domains (supply chain, factories, containers, projects, finance, nurses, conference boxes, etc.).

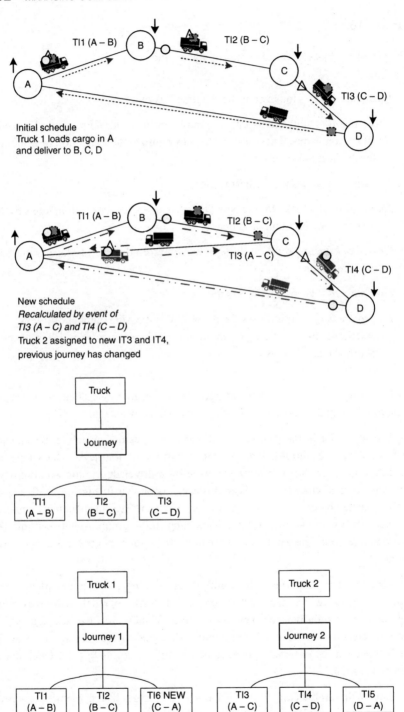

Figure 22: Multi-level virtual world architecture.

Every agent is given the task of obtaining the best possible match for its client and a right to drop a previously agreed match if a better opportunity presents itself as events continue occurring. The abandoned partner proactively seeks a new match.

Agents in the virtual world use the enhanced contract net negotiations protocol. Within contract net protocol agents pass the following iterations:

- Ask for pre-matching (rough) estimation
- Ask for plan, if possible to allocate without drop
- Ask for complete plan (drop is allowed)
- Accept proposal
- Receive notification that plan is applied/failed

At each stage agents can cut or prioritise negotiation branches, thus detecting uninteresting options with fewer calculations.

If a plan fails, the agent can re-send a modified proposal.

If an agent has two equal options, one of which involves drop and another is without drop – it will prefer the option without drop, as it allows saving system time.

The protocol is decomposed into two parts: the contractor role and coordinator role. The contractor role is responsible for (and fully encapsulates) message exchanges between a particular pair of agents representing demand and resource.

Coordinator role contains decision-making logic of an agent at the protocol level and allows the demand agent to interact with several resources simultaneously (demand agent's coordinator role) and resource agent – with several demands (resource agent's coordinator role).

Agents have multiple objectives, or criteria (quality, price, time, risk) each with a weight coefficient. This can be changed by the user for each individual agent. At any moment of time the user can increase the relative importance of the service level or maximise profit criterion. If for example orders from VIP customers are allocated and a new order comes from an even more important customer with tighter conditions, this may result in decreasing the service level for already allocated orders within the allowable interval. Changes in weight coefficients represent the change of agent strategy of working in the virtual world.

Each order finds out the cost of its transportation using price list and finds the most profitable journey. The profit received from transportation is shared between TI, journey and truck agents. The microeconomics includes a system of taxation aimed to further improve scheduling efficiency. It does this by applying a penalty (tax) for making changes to the schedule close to commit time. This ensures that only changes giving significant benefits are made as planning time runs out.

The initial scene, which is a model of the transportation system at the beginning of scheduling, is constructed by an operator using a user-friendly editor or imported from an XML file. The scene depicts all transportation resources (trucks, trailers, depots, warehouses, loading points, delivery points) and their locations on the transportation network. Goals, criteria, objectives (KPI), strategies and preferences are specified.

As the first order arrives, agents split the order into TIs and allocate transportation resources to each TI. The initial scene is thus modified into the current scene, which is being updated after every event. The current schedule is extracted from the current scene and can take the form of a table or a diagram.

New events are added to the current schedule. They can be imported from third-party systems, from XML files or added manually. Events are assigned individual objectives and strategies. When new events are entered into the system, the system stops other activities (or delays the incoming event) and starts TI allocation.

If events are entered in a batch, prioritisation is carried out. Outstanding TIs can be prioritised with the help of prioritisation logic defined in ontology or manually.

Next, new TIs are planned incrementally. TI agents pre-match by making rough option estimation and checking constraints. Next, they start negotiation with journey agents, telling them the amount they are ready to pay for the allocation. If a TI is of interest to the journey, it tries to allocate this TI using open slot, shift or drop algorithms. If an option is found, journey makes the final option estimation and checks constraints. Journey sends message to TI to confirm allocation and informs other TIs belonging to it that new TI was allocated and they can re-calculate their values and costs.

If there are no new events, dissatisfied TI, journey, driver shift and truck agents could start proactive improvement of their allocation. An important advantage of software is that this proactive improvement takes place in the system whenever possible – the scheduler continuously works towards the best possible schedule. Any type of agent can be proactive and agents who are dissatisfied with their current allocation are most likely to get proactive.

User can review results using a Gantt chart or a map and analyse reports. There is a possibility to manually adjust the schedule asking the system to suggest alternatives. The system can also highlight parts of the schedule that needs improving.

Each journey has its individual commit time. As commit time approaches, the agents get more and more active to utilise the last chance to find a better option. After start of a journey's commit time (e.g., 3 hours before the driver should set off) no further changes are made to this journey's schedule – journey is passed to commit stage. In the initial version committed journeys' schedules could not be changed.

The incremental nature of our scheduling and the use of a variety of planning strategies mean that the scheduler will always produce a plan for an order, even if it is entered into the system very shortly before its commit time.

Human operators are provided with facilities for monitoring the scheduling process and overruling the decisions made by agents. The scheduler supports users in their interaction with the system by providing them with options and evaluating consequences of their decisions.

Connecting Virtual and Real Worlds

Disruptive events, which occur in real world, are communicated to virtual world (the system), as follows: orders are entered into the system as they arrive, failures of resources are either entered by operators or sent as text messages from driver's mobile phones and positions of trucks are detected by GPS. Messages from virtual world to real world, i.e., instructions to drivers, loaders, etc., are sent by text messages or emails.

Results

The first version of the scheduler was tested on two sets of real-life data obtained from Client A (a third-party logistics provider) and Client B (a provider of logistics and freight management services).

Client A requirements were to create transportation schedules in real time for 200 TIs and 50 trucks (36 own fleet trucks plus 15 third-party carriers) operating on the UK business network. The network included nine distribution centres/factories, cross-dock points for primary/secondary moves consolidation, three truck bases doing shared operations. In addition to requirements discussed earlier client specified handling TI availability windows, backhaul, consolidation, vehicle capacity availability windows and constraint stressing.

Client B requirements were to create transportation schedules for 4,000 TIs and 200 trucks operating on the UK business network. The network included primary and secondary deliveries between about 600 locations, 3 cross-docks, 4 secure trailer swap locations and other types of locations. The network was also characterised by considerable number of very small orders.

Special requirements included dynamic routing, cross-docking, handling location availability windows and driver breaks.

The scheduler has completed a schedule for 200 TIs in 8 minutes, planning 116 journeys of a total of 20,790 miles. The quality compares well with the results of the current process, which requires several hours to produce a schedule and has two dispatchers working on the basis of a plan day_1 for day_3 execution. With the scheduler it would be feasible to plan day_1 for day_2 execution, or even day_1 for day_1 execution.

For 4,000 orders with dynamical routing through three cross-docks it took the scheduler about 4 hours to build a schedule. This schedule shows strong consolidation of small orders onto trucks. It is also capable of incrementally planning new orders in near real time (a few seconds for a new order). As far as we know, this has not been achieved by any other transportation scheduling system.

9

Adaptive data mining

The Problem

The main limitations of current data mining software are that it cannot mine data that perpetually change and that the user is required to make a hypothesis that certain patterns exist before the procedure can even start.

There are however many important situations where data is arriving for analysis in small batches at frequent, unpredictable intervals. Perhaps the most interesting example is an Internet portal with a large number of visitors who leave behind a small but significant amount of data whenever they visit the site. To extract a coherent and up-to-date pattern of behaviour of customers, it is essential to ensure that the mining process is dynamic, i.e., capable of taking into account data as it arrives. Current pattern discovery and data mining algorithms cannot cope with these conditions.

The Solution

Brief Overview

The discovery of patterns in data is, basically, an adaptive allocation of data to clusters. The process of allocation is simpler than in logistics because the space and time are irrelevant. The complexity is caused by the unpredictable arrival of data and a variety of data formats.

We have developed a new method for the dynamic pattern discovery [19,20]. It has been implemented by ontology-based multi-agent technology and it works autonomously. There is no need for users to start the data mining process by proposing hypotheses.

Fundamental Concepts

The most important concepts involved in this method are defined below.

> Data clusters are groups of data elements (records) with common features, e.g., records of all customers purchasing bread and milk on a daily basis.

Such data cluster represents a pattern of behaviour of customers and can be used for managing customer relations.

Data clustering is a process by which data elements are grouped into *clusters* according to a set of given clustering criteria.

Dynamic data clustering is a process where the data set that is being clustered changes during the clustering process in an unpredictable manner.

Clustering propensity is the capability of record agents to proactively search for clustering partners. To achieve clustering propensity each data element is assigned a certain *energy level*.

The energy level of a record or a cluster, measured in terms of agreed energy units (eu), determines the ability of a record or a cluster to search for the optimal clustering option and thus its ability to impact the process of self-organisation (changing clustering configurations). The concept of energy level is also used to limit the time required to accomplish an acceptable clustering solution. Energy levels could be distributed to records equally or by some domain-dependent rules. For example, in e-commerce applications, the energy level available to a record can be set as a commission for each item sold. Then the record of a sale of a batch of goods would be richer than a record of a sale of one item. In general, data elements that are more important for the users are given higher energy levels. It works as follows. Data elements spend their energy by paying for joining/forming/leaving clusters. Important data elements, i.e., those with higher energy can enter into a greater number of clustering negotiations with a view to attaining the optimal clustering membership. In contrast, data elements of lesser importance will be limited to a smaller number of searches. Clusters attracting more important data elements accumulate large energy levels and are therefore more visible to the users.

Clustering criteria help agents to decide how to group records together.

Cluster valuation formulae specify how exactly a cluster value is to be assessed by record agents. In general, the cluster value depends on the number of data elements belonging to the cluster, the energy levels of data members, the shape (or boundaries) of the cluster, the number of attributes of the cluster, their variety, etc. A simple and effective way of determining a cluster value is to equate it to the density of the cluster. If we represent data elements belonging to a cluster in an N-dimensional space, where N is the number of attributes in the data set, we can define cluster density as the number of data elements within the cluster volume.

Record valuation formulae specify how exactly a record value is to be assessed by cluster agents. If cluster density is to be maximised, then data elements that increase the density will be preferred.

System value is the value of the overall clustering process. The guiding principle for the allocation of data elements to clusters is to maximise the system value.

How the Dynamic Data Mining Works

Let us assume that an MAS is given a task of allocating records to clusters and that those records arrive to the system in small batches. Times of arrival of records and their features are unpredictable.

Then, the dynamic data clustering method is as follows:

1. An agent is allocated to a new record as it arrives to the system.

2. The new record agent considers available clusters, selects those that appear attractive (as determined by a cluster valuation formula) and sends to the appropriate cluster agents' applications for membership.

3. Cluster agents, which receive membership applications, evaluate the applicants using a record valuation formula. Those cluster agents that decide that the new applicant will increase the energy level of their clusters send membership offers to the applicants.

4. The record agent accepts the most appropriate offer and joins a cluster.

5. If no suitable cluster is available, the record agent attempts to form a new cluster with other records, which may or may not belong to clusters, by sending cluster formation proposals to their agents.

6. The record agents, to which formation of new clusters is proposed, consider the offer. They accept the offer only if it increases the overall value of the system. By accepting the offer agents effectively reorganise the whole system – the previously established relationships between the released records and their clusters are destroyed and new relationships between different records are established increasing the overall value of the system (the process of self-organisation).

7. Agents representing newly created clusters and/or clusters whose properties (value, boundaries, number of records) have changed during the self-organisation, start a new negotiation round with agents of selected records, repeating the process as described above.

8. The clustering process continues until all records are linked to clusters and no change of cluster membership can increase the value of the system, or until the time available for clustering is exhausted.

9. Under conditions of perpetual arrival of new data elements to the system, at some point in the clustering process agents will begin dropping out-of-date data elements from further clustering considerations (the process known as evolution).

The clustering resembles a crystallisation processes – records create clusters (structures) and these structures, in turn, participate in the formation of more complex structures. The process stops when the whole domain is clusterised (crystallised). The outcome of the process is the creation of high-level structures.

An Example

We have four records (data elements), which arrive to the system one by one (Fig. 23). They are Record 1 (2,4), Record 2 (3,3), Record 3 (6,3) and Record 4 (7,3). The cluster valuation formula is based on the density of clusters and the negotiation rule is "first consider the nearest data element or cluster".

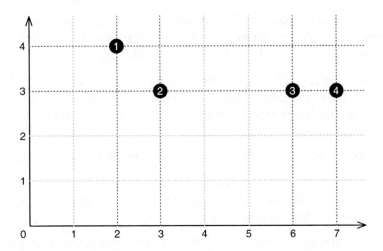

Figure 23:   Data elements available for clustering.

Then the clustering steps will be as follows:

(a) Record 1 arrives to the system.

(b) Record 2 arrives to the system. It forms with Record 1 a new cluster, Cluster 5 (Fig. 24).

(c) Record 3 arrives to the system. It applies to Cluster 5 for membership but it is rejected because its membership would reduce the cluster density. Record 3 then suggests to Cluster 5 to form a new cluster, which would include Record 3 and Cluster 5. They agree and form Cluster 6 (Fig. 25).

(d) Record 4 arrives to the system. Record 4 suggests to Record 3 to leave Cluster 6 and join Record 4 in a new cluster. Record 3 agrees because the new cluster would have a greater density than Cluster 6. Cluster 6 is destroyed and Cluster 7 is created from Records 3 and 4 (Fig. 26).

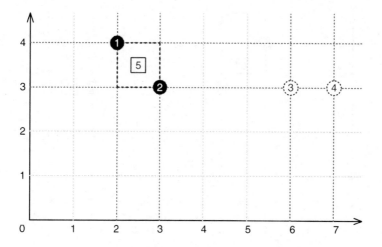

Figure 24: Records 1 and 2 form cluster 5.

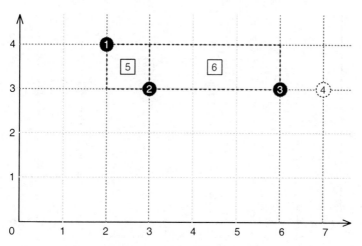

Figure 25: Record 3 and cluster 5 form cluster 6.

(e) Cluster 7 then proposes to Cluster 5 to form together a new cluster. They form
     Cluster 8 (Fig. 27).

Microeconomics of Clustering

Agents representing data elements and clusters negotiate cluster memberships
according to one of several available models.

The Club Model

Data elements pay membership fees to join clusters. Fees are fixed.

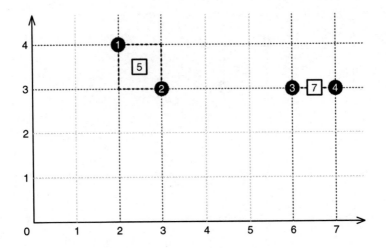

Figure 26: Cluster 6 is destroyed; cluster 7 is formed.

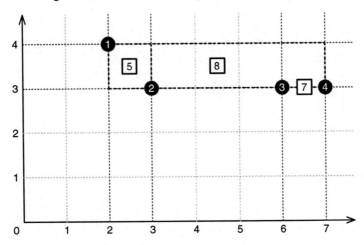

Figure 27: Clusters 5 and 7 form Cluster 8.

The Shareholder Model

Data elements purchase shares in clusters. Share prices depend on the number of data elements belonging to a cluster and their energy levels and may vary in time. Data elements have opportunities to increase their energy levels by entering or quitting a cluster at an opportune time. They can also lose energy if they make a wrong clustering decision. This model increases differentiation between clusters from the point of view of their usefulness to users.

The Tax Model

Data elements pay a tax during their membership in clusters. This model enables evolutionary changes in the system because data elements are forced to quit when they exhaust their energy levels and leave vacancies for newly arriving data. Differences in energy levels of data elements provide a mechanism for selection. This model encourages data elements as well as clusters to consider their long-term prospects when they make clustering choices. For example, a cluster that does not attract candidates for membership may decide to reduce its membership tax to bring in new members and thus prolong its life.

How Clustering Depends on the Model

Data clustering and clustering results depend on the selected model of cluster membership. In particular, the following cluster features are dependent on the clustering criteria: (a) the size of clusters – a large number of small clusters or a smaller number of large clusters; (b) equality (all records are of equal importance) versus elitism (some records are given preferences) and (c) speed of clustering.

Consider the following example (Table 6).

Table 6: Records Available for Clustering.

BUYER'S NAME	GOODS PURCHASED	PURCHASE VALUE IN EU
Smith	Potatoes	500
Jones	Tomatoes	13
Ford	Potatoes	10
Philips	Potatoes	700
Denham	Cucumbers	20

If the club model is used and cluster membership fee is set to 3 eu, and all records are given equal amount of money, say 10 eu, the system will generate the following two clusters (Table 7).

Table 7: Two Clusters Produced by the Club Model.

CLUSTER NAME	CLUSTER MEMBERS	MEMBERSHIP COST	CLUSTER ENERGY LEVEL
A Potatoes	Smith Ford Philips	3	9
B Vegetables	Smith Jones Philips Ford Denham	3	15

Now let us consider the shareholder model. We shall assume that each data element has the amount of eu equal to the purchase value and that the amount of eu for participation in the cluster is calculated in the following way (Table 8).

Table 8: Two Clusters Produced by the Shareholder Model.

CLUSTER NAME	CLUSTER MEMBERS	MEMBERS COST	CLUSTER ENERGY LEVEL
A Potatoes	Smith Philips	60	120
B Vegetables	Jones Ford Denham	2	6

First record (Smith) can create a cluster A, called potatoes, for 10% of overall money (50 eu). Now when Philips arrives to the system he can decide whether to pay the same sum of 50 eu or a larger sum, say, 10% of his own overall money (70 eu). In the latter case he will receive a larger number of cluster shares (which could be later sold when the cluster becomes richer and the record decides to leave the cluster and join another).

The average cost of entering the cluster is $(50 + 70)/2 = 60$ eu.

It is not profitable for richer clusters to be shareholders of clusters with a small entrance fee because they are poor.

We see here a dramatic difference in the way the two clusters are formed. The shareholder model clearly separates rich records from the poor.

And what is the difference for the client? The first model is useful if users wish to know which customer purchases what kind of vegetables and the second model can tell the client who purchases certain goods in big quantities. The two models may help the client to launch two different focused advertising campaigns.

To summarise, the club model promotes equality and creates a larger number of clusters in earlier stages (because the membership fee is low and fixed, and it is, therefore, easier to create a new cluster); once in a cluster, data elements are reluctant to change their membership (because the energy level of new records is not sufficient to initiate the restructuring of clusters).

The shareholder model promotes elitism and individualisation; it produces a clear separation of rich and poor data elements, generates a smaller number of clusters, enables a greater mobility of data elements even in the later stages (because new rich records can force the restructuring of clusters, even ousting poorer records from rich clusters) and sets a higher speed of clustering (because the number of options available to each data element is reduced considerably – the high entrance costs prevent poor data elements to join rich clusters).

The tax model gives additional dimension to the clustering process. When the records have to pay money to stay in the system the structure of clusters changes with time as impoverished records are forced to leave. The tax model is normally used alongside either of the other two models to induce evolution of clusters.

Representation of Clusters

A clustering problem domain is usefully represented as a data table, where each row is a record and columns contain field values. Such a table could be regarded as a multidimensional space, where each record is an element of this space. In general, the space is heterogeneous, since axes of the space can be of different types (integer, real, etc.). Clustering is then a process of detecting dense concentration of elements within the problem domain space. A cluster is defined by a set of axes in the multidimensional space and by limits on each of this axes within which all elements belonging to the cluster are located. A data element (record) can belong to several clusters, which means that boundaries of segments of multidimensional spaces representing clusters can intersect.

It is often very convenient to represent clusters as rules of the type:

> IF (condition A1) and (condition A2) and … (condition An), THEN (condition B1) and (condition B2) and … (condition Bm).

where Ai are conditions which include fields over which we have no control (independent fields) and Bi are conditions, which include fields, whose values is permissible to manipulate. An example of such a rule is "If an order requires transportation of a cargo of 5 kg, then this order should be allocated to the trucks of type GMC that belong to Trans Carrier company".

To produce a rule from the description of a cluster as a segment in a multidimensional space, all axes of the space have to be divided into two groups – one containing fields over which we have control and which we can manipulate and the other containing fields which are given (and cannot be changed). Then, dependencies of fields from the first category upon fields from the second category (known as patterns) have to be determined. Clusters constructed over axes which all belong to a single category are ignored. Clustering procedure may omit values along certain axes in which case the cluster is defined over a sub-dimension of the whole space.

Note that a rule derived as described above always represents a cluster and therefore, if a clustering procedure discovered all clusters, it discovered all rules. The inverse statement is not generally true – a cluster cannot be always represented by a rule, e.g., when the cluster has elements all belonging to a single category (all independent or all dependent).

Rules are evaluated using the following three criteria:

1. *Representativeness* shows how many elements of a cluster are included into a rule. This parameter does not depend upon the patterns.

2. *Confidence level* shows how many elements of a cluster that are included into the left part of the rule (IF part) do not meet conditions of the right part of the rule (THEN part). This parameter depends upon the pattern inherent in the cluster. For example, the pattern "among all ones that are parous, all are women" has a confidence level of 100% while a reverse rule has a low confidence level because "not all women are parous".

3. *Completeness* shows how many elements of a cluster that meet conditions of the right part of the rule (THEN part) do not meet conditions of the left part of the rule (IF part). For example, the rule "if you are a human being, then you are mortal" has high level of representativeness but low level of completeness (since not all mortal beings are human beings).

The higher the value of representativeness and of confidence level, the more valuable the revealed interdependency of cluster elements.

When a rule is derived, we can try to move conditions from the IF part of the rule to the THEN part of the rule. If this operation does not decrease the confidence level of the rule, then the modified rule is more useful. For example, the rule "If an order requires transportation from Krasnoyarsk then destination location is Moscow and the order should be assigned to truck of type ZIL" is more useful than the rule "If an order requires transportation from Krasnoyarsk to Moscow, then this order should be assigned to truck of type ZIL", provided that the confidence level has not been decreased by the operation.

Application Examples

Transportation Scheduling

A logistics company required a tool capable of generating automatically a schedule that would be similar to the schedule produced manually by an experienced operator. The customer did not define metric criteria to estimate proximity and similarity of schedules and therefore the evaluation of results was done by an expert.

The customer provided a data set of 920 transportation orders that were scheduled in the past manually.

The first task was the extraction of hidden rules from the data set provided by the customer. For this purpose a table was created with each row representing an order.

The multi-agent Pattern Discovery Tool found 218 rules. More than half of the rules had the confidence level of 100%, which testifies to the effectiveness of the Tool.

Rules discovered by the system were shown to an expert who confirmed most of the rules and agreed that the discovered dependencies are intrinsic characteristics of the problem domain. Moreover, the expert declared that 8% of the discovered rules were not known before the system discovered them and that these rules had a great confidence level value.

The discovered rules were then loaded into the knowledge base of an agent-based scheduler with a view to performing a comparison between (a) a schedule produced by the scheduler without extracted rules; (b) a schedule produced by the scheduler with extracted rules loaded and (c) a schedule produced manually by an experienced operator.

Test runs were executed on a data set different from the one from which rules were extracted and each test run was based on 1-week operation. The loading of extracted rules increased the speed of automatic scheduling considerably: 3 hours with rules versus 5 hours without rules. The schedule produced with the help of rules was more like the schedule produced manually by an experienced operator than the schedule produced without rules.

The loading of extracted rules into the scheduler improved the quality of the resulting schedule, which was quantified as follows: (a) manual rework needed decreased by 32%; (b) journey quality increased by 17%; (c) the presence of gaps in the journeys decreased by 11%; (d) fleet mileage decreased by 16%; (e) fleet usage decreased by 8%; (f) estimated time required for customisation of schedules dramatically decreased from 1–2 months to 10–15 days.

Finding possible options for consolidation in transportation logistics is one of the very useful applications of clustering and clustering analysis. For this purpose appropriate filters are devised for IF and THEN parts of the rules to pass only those fields that are relevant for the problem at hand; geographical coordinates, time windows and journey–time matrix information are normally of particular interest. Each cluster passed through the filter can be considered as a group of orders that are potentially amenable to consolidation.

At the next step it is necessary to define for each cluster the way in which consolidation should be applied – whether all orders in the group are to be shipped by one truck or by several trucks that are similar in characteristics. The decision depends upon the distance between locations, since time is required to load and deliver each cargo, whilst driver's working hours are strictly limited. The decision also depends upon cargo properties as in some cases a special-purpose truck may be required to deliver a cargo, for example, of chilled goods. Additional clustering run on the consolidation clusters helps to bring to light more dependencies and details.

Creating Insurance Templates

Our client, one of the five biggest insurance companies in the UK, had the following problem. Since car insurance premiums depend on many parameters, including client's gender and age, their education level, yearly income, class of the car and driving history, their lawyers created over the last 20 years more than 25,000 documents related to car insurance contracts. The task given to our team was to analyse these documents, classify them according to their semantic similarity and create a contract template for each group of documents. Contract templates were expected to include the most frequent clauses from the constituent documents within the group to be used in future as a basis for all new contracts. A part of the task was also to analyse and classify available contracts from the competitive insurance companies and take these results into account during the creation of templates. The initial estimate was that there would be around 100 groups of documents and that the whole work would take approximately 16 man-years of highly qualified law experts. Our task was to automate this process thus saving time and money.

The solution to this problem, developed by our team [20], was based on the multi-agent clustering method described earlier, combined with text processing described in the next chapter.

First, semantic processing system was used to represent the document meaning as a semantic network; then, our multi-agent clustering method was applied to classify documents; and, finally, a heuristic method was developed to create templates based on groups of semantically similar documents.

Forecasting

A travel agent had statistics on their customers that included personal information, travel history (previously visited country) and the country customers plan to visit next. The last item was often missing because not all customers articulated their plans when visiting the travel agent website. The task was to help the travel agent to forecast future destinations for their customers by discovering patterns in the following data set.

From available data it was easy to derive rules that predict behaviour of customers such as IF age range = "18–30", previous destination = "France" THEN the new destination = "Netherlands". The pattern informs the company that it can expect customers from group 3293 to book their next visit to Netherlands.

Fraud/Error Detection

Fraud/error detection is a process of identifying abnormalities or unusual activities in data sets, in other words, situations that deviate from general trends. It is important and sometimes vital to consider all unusual cases, since they can represent either intentional fraud or a data entry error. For example, if most vehicles in a pool are charged from $10 to $25 for parking while two trucks pay $200, there are at least two explanations for this discrepancy: a computer operator accidentally entered an additional zero, or a person in charge diverted some funds to his account and attempted to cover this fraud with false parking charges. Our Multi-Agent Pattern Discovery system identifying all cases where the value of an attribute in the THEN part of a rule deviated from the anticipated value.

Results

In all applications described above the multi-agent method of adaptive clustering succeeded in solving clients' problems to their satisfaction. In one case, our system saved 16 man-years of highly qualified law expert effort.

No comparison of our method with other approaches was possible because no conventional computational method was used or applicable.

10

Adaptive semantic processing

The Problem

The Internet is a vast digital *network of computers* spreading around the globe. As stated in Chapter 1, at the time of writing 3 billion people used the Internet, which is more than 40% of the total number of people on the planet. One could argue that almost a half of all people who populate the Earth live in a *global village* – they can rapidly communicate with each other, exchange gossip, show photos, trade, provide services and ask each other for help.

The real breakthrough in establishing a useful global network came with the invention of the World Wide Web by Tim Berners-Lee in 1989. The Web is a *network of documents* in a standard format, stored on interconnected computers. In 2008 it was established that the Web, which can be indexed, contains at least 63 billion web pages and Google announced that their search engine had discovered 1 trillion unique page addresses. The significance of the Web is that it enables documents to be linked directly irrespective of their location.

The third stage in moving towards a true global village is well under way. The idea is to build a *network of content* stored on the web – the *Semantic Web* – making it possible for machines to correctly interpret meaning of data and text, and to meaningfully answer queries from people and machines.

Semantics is the study of meaning in communication. The word derives from Greek semantikos "significant", from *semaino* "to signify, to indicate" and from *sema* "sign, mark, token". In linguistics it is a study of interpretation of signs as used by agents or communities within particular circumstances and contexts. It has related meanings in several other fields.

Tim Berners-Lee originally expressed his vision of the Semantic Web as follows:

> I have a dream for the Web [in which computers] become capable of analysing all the data on the Web – the content, links, and transactions between people and computers. A "Semantic Web", which should make this possible, has yet to emerge, but when it does, the day-to-day mechanisms of trade, bureaucracy and our daily lives will be handled by machines talking to machines. The 'intelligent agents' people have touted for ages will finally materialise (Tim Berners-Lee, 1999).

Possible applications of semantic processing are numerous and include:

- Written communication between people and computers
- Written communication among computers
- Software translators
- Text referencing engines
- Semantic search engines
- Auto-abstracting engines
- Annotation and classification systems
- Semantic document-flow management systems

Despite a considerable research effort in areas such as computer linguistics, artificial intelligence and neural networks the problem of text understanding by computers has not been effectively solved. The reason may well be that the currently proposed solutions to this problem are largely centralised, sequential and static.

The Solution

Brief Overview

Semantic processing is best formulated as an adaptive allocation of meanings to words and sentences. The whole text that needs to be interpreted is given in advance. Nevertheless, the allocation process advances step by step and at each step the previously agreed match is re-examined and may be changed [21]. The allocation process resembles self-organisation. The complexity is caused by the number of meanings that could match each word, depending on context.

The main idea of the approach employed in our solution is that a software agent is assigned to each word of the text under consideration. Agents have access to a comprehensive repository of knowledge about possible meanings of words in the text and engage into negotiation with each other until a consensus is reached on meanings of each word and each sentence. In some cases the method may discover several contradictory meanings of a sentence. The conflict is then resolved by an agent-triggered consultation with the user and consequent updating of the repository of knowledge. To simplify the process of extracting meanings, the method performs an initial morphological and syntactic analysis of the text.

Fundamentals

An adaptive semantic processing system was developed by our team, capable of assessing content of scientific abstracts in the domain of human genome decoding.

Key concepts of the method employed are as follows:

A syntactic descriptor is a network of words linked by syntactic relations representing a grammatically correct sentence.

A semantic descriptor is a network of grammatically and semantically compatible words, which represents a computer readable interpretation of the meaning of a text. If semantic ontology describes all possible meanings of words in a domain, a semantic descriptor describes the meaning of a particular text.

Self-organisation is the capability of a system to autonomously, i.e., without human intervention, modify existing and/or establish new relationships among its components with a view to increasing a given value or recovering from a disturbance, such as an unexpected addition or subtraction of a component. In the context of text understanding any autonomous change of a link between two agents representing a meaning and a word is considered as a step in the process of self-organisation.

Evolution is the capability of a system to autonomously modify its components and/or links in response, or in anticipation of changes in its environment. In the context of text understanding any autonomous update of ontology based on the newly acquired information is considered as a step in the process of evolution.

The Agent-Based Method for Semantic Processing

The new method for semantic processing was employed in designing our solution, which consists of the following four steps:

1. Morphological analysis

2. Syntactic analysis

3. Semantic analysis

4. Pragmatics

The text is divided into sentences. Sentences are fed into the meaning extraction process one by one.

Morphological Analysis

1. An agent is assigned to each word in the sentence.

2. Word agents access ontology and acquire relevant knowledge on morphology.

3. Word agents execute morphological analysis of the sentence and establish characteristics of each word, such as gender, number, case and time.

4. If morphological analysis results in polysemy, i.e., a situation in which some words could play several roles in a sentence (a noun or adjective or verb), several agents are assigned to the same word, each representing one of its possible roles.

Syntactical Analysis

5. Word agents access ontology and acquire relevant knowledge on syntax.

6. Word agents execute syntactical analysis where they aim at identifying the syntactical structure of the sentence. For example, a subject searches for a predicate of the same gender and number, and a predicate looks for a suitable subject and objects. Conflicts are resolved through a process of negotiation. A grammatically correct sentence is represented by means of a syntactic descriptor.

7. If results of the syntactical analysis are ambiguous, i.e., several variants of the syntactic structure of the sentence under consideration are feasible, each feasible variant is represented by a different syntactic descriptor.

Semantic Analysis

8. Word agents access ontology and acquire relevant knowledge on semantics.

9. Each grammatically correct version of the sentence under consideration is subjected to semantic analysis. This analysis is aimed at establishing the semantic compatibility of words in each grammatically correct sentence. Word agents learn from ontology possible meanings of words that they represent and by consulting each other attempt to eliminate inappropriate alternatives.

10. Once agents agree on a grammatically and semantically correct sentence; they create a semantic descriptor of the sentence, which is a network of concepts and values contained in the sentence.

11. If a solution that satisfies all agents cannot be found, agents compose a message to the user explaining the difficulties and suggesting how the issues could be resolved.

12. Each new grammatically and semantically correct sentence generated by the steps 1–11 is checked for semantic compatibility with semantic descriptors of preceding sentences. In the process agents may decide to modify previously agreed semantic interpretations of words or sentences (self-organisation).

13. When all sentences are processed, the final semantic descriptor of the whole document is constructed thus providing a computer readable semantic interpretation of the text.

Pragmatics

14. Word agents access ontology and acquire relevant knowledge on pragmatics, which is closely related to the application at hand.

15. At this stage agents consider their application-oriented tasks and decide if they need to execute any additional processes. For example, if the application is a Person–Computer Dialog, agents may decide that they need to ask the user to supply some additional information; if the application is a Search Engine, agents will compare the semantic descriptor of the search request with semantic descriptors of available search results. If the application is a Classifier, agents will compare semantic descriptors of different documents and form groups of documents with semantic proximity.

Salient Features of the Solution

Let us recapitulate main features of the proposed method:

- Decision-making rules are specified in ontology, which incorporates general knowledge on text understanding, language-oriented rules and specific knowledge on the problem domain.
- Every word in the text under consideration is given the opportunity to autonomously and proactively search for its own meaning using knowledge available in ontology.
- Tentative decisions are reached through a process of consultation and negotiation among all word agents.
- The final decision on the meaning of every word is reached through a consensus among all word agents.
- Semantic descriptors are produced for individual sentences and for the whole text.
- The extraction of meanings follows an autonomous trial-and-error pattern (self-organisation).
- The process of meaning extraction can be regulated by modifying ontology.

Application Example: Assessing Relevance of Abstracts

During the rush to decode human genome the progress was so rapid and competition so fears that researchers working in private, small research labs could not find time to read abstracts of daily published newspapers claiming new discoveries and yet being well informed was vital for success. The need emerged for a system capable of reading rapidly large numbers of abstracts and assessing their relevance to research at hand.

The above method has been applied to the problem of searching for relevant abstracts, as described below through a series of illustrations.

Fig. 28 shows a published abstract of a scientific paper, which needs to be converted into a computer readable format.

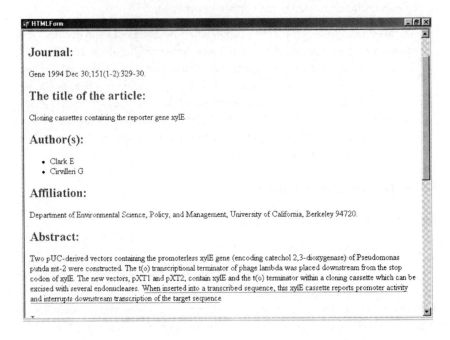

Figure 28: An abstract selected for semantic processing.

The semantic descriptor of the title of the abstract is shown in Fig. 29. Note that the sentence has been completely understood by the system – the relations between the gene and locus and gene properties have been determined. Note that their meanings are shown at the bottom of the screen (in biology a locus by definition is a specific site of the particular gene or chromosome; according to domain ontology "cloning cassette" is a synonym of the semantic concept "locus").

Fig. 30 shows how a tentative semantic descriptor of the whole text is modified during semantic analysis in a stepwise manner (self-organisation). Blue links indicate connections that were added to the semantic descriptor during the analysis of the last sentence of the text (the underlined sentence from Fig. 28). As a result of the analysis of the last sentence the system discovered some new concepts and new relations between the existing nodes of the descriptor, including a new relation "Have" between the gene and the locus; furthermore, the gene has obtained a new "Insert" relation and the relation "Have" has been established between the locus and the new node, "operon" (in biology operon by definition is a controllable unit of transcription consisting of a number of structural genes transcribed together; it contains at least two distinct regions: the operator and the promoter; therefore, according to ontology and the text of the abstract, the semantic descriptor includes the concept "operon").

The final semantic descriptor of the whole abstract is shown in Fig. 31.

In addition to creating semantic descriptors for each abstract it is necessary to formulate a semantic descriptor of the query. Fig. 32 shows a semantic descriptor of a request to search for abstracts in which an organism is connected with a sequence through the relation "Have".

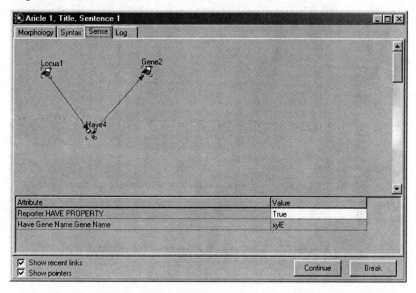

Figure 29: Semantic descriptors of the title.

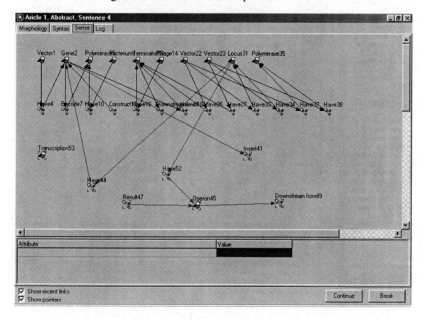

Figure 30: Semantic descriptors of the text.

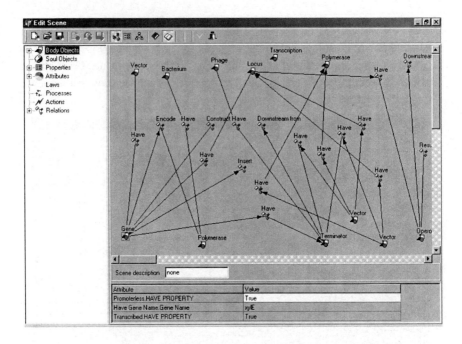

Figure 31: Semantic descriptor of the abstract.

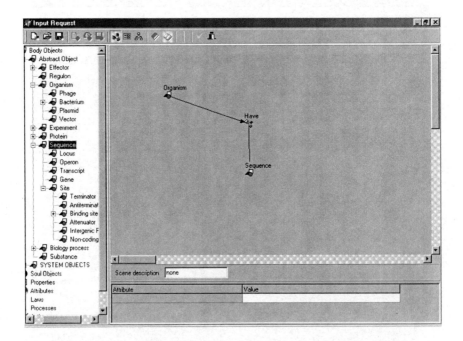

Figure 32: A request to search for abstracts with a particular content.

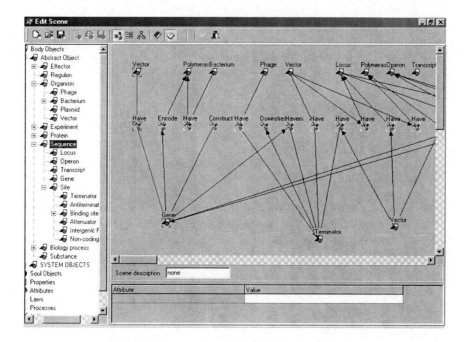

Figure 33:   Comparison of semantic descriptors of abstracts.

Results

Results of our effort to produce software capable of reading and interpreting meaning of text *in a narrow domain* exceeded all expectations. The system was used by research teams in anger and achieved considerable savings of abstract assessing effort.

The problem of Semantic Web though will be solved only by a considerable expansion of semantic processing ontology, which would have to cover a vast span of knowledge imbedded into the Web.

11

Adaptive detection of clashes caused by design changes

The Problem

During the collaborative design of a very large mechanical structure such as an airplane wing, which, for a very large aircraft, consists of more than 10,000 parts, there is a frequent need for design changes.

The problem is that changing position or dimensions of one wing component may lead to the whole chain of modifications to neighbouring components to ensure that they fit perfectly together. The current practice is to identify design conflicts once a month by a clash-analysis program running on a grid of powerful machines and requiring about 2 weeks to check all possible clashes for the complete wing. The procedure is to check every component against every other component irrespective if they are mutually connected or not, which generates a huge volume of data for processing. The problem is even more complex if the clash analysis includes electric, magnetic, stressing and other aspects of design.

The Solution

Brief Overview

Analysis of clashes after a designer changes position or size of an aircraft wing component can be formulated as adaptive allocation of changes to components. All clashes are identified in real time – between the two consecutive design changes. The source of complexity is the number of components potentially affected by a design change.

We have solved this problem by developing a pilot knowledge-driven MAS, which is capable of rapidly detecting components "next to" the component that has been changed. Component agents exchange messages searching for components that can be affected after every design change, as it occurs, in real time.

The prototype MAS for checking and eliminating clashes caused by aircraft wing design changes was tested on real data and demonstrated dramatic improvements in comparison with conventional methods.

Knowledge Base

The wing ontology was constructed using ontology management toolset with classes of wing components as nodes and relations, including "neighbourhood", as links. Using the same toolset a scene was constructed for the specific wing, which contained more than 1.5 million object instances and relations. It was possible to load into the scene only objects from the existing CAD system and relations only of the type "part-of". Even that was sufficient to establish a network of wing object instances and relations of the type "neighbour".

Virtual World

Every wing component that was subjected to redesign was immediately checked for clashes. This was done by creating an agent for the altered component with the task to compare component sizes prior and post redesign and to find all wing components that may be affected by the change. Searching the wing scene for neighbour relations yielded rapid identification of potential clashes. An agent is then assigned to each identified neighbouring component with the task to evaluate further implications of redesign. The wave of newly created agents, each evaluating the implications of changes, can spread across the scene in all directions and agents can carry out evaluations in parallel and asynchronously. If a design change does not affect a neighbour, the wave in the corresponding direction of the wing scene fades.

The procedure for checking clashes is explained on an example of a wing design scene as shown in Fig. 34.

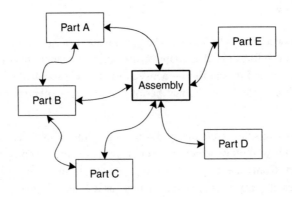

Figure 34: A fragment of aircraft wing design scene.

The system is triggered by any change in the wing design. Let's assume that the size of part C is changed.

- System creates, or wakes up, Part-C Agent.
- The new agent investigates the current scene, which is a network of parts, and finds that it has one neighbour, Part B.
- Part-C Agent creates Part-B Agent and informs him of changes of Part C size and its new boundaries.
- Part-B Agent compares new and old sizes, or position, of Part C, and also check its boundaries according to the type of their relations.
- If changes, which initiated the search for possible clashes, are not affecting Part B and there are no risks, this is the end of the ripple of changes.
- If Part B is affected, its agent identifies the conflict and either asks user to validate the situation, or autonomously changes Part B size appropriately.
- The process is repeated for other neighbours in the wing design scene, Part A, Part E, Part D.

The above process represents an "autonomous adaptation of the wing design", or, in other words, "wing design self-organisation", which progresses through the design scene as a ripple effect triggered by the initial change carried out by a designer.

Results

Our prototype dramatically reduced the processing effort in comparison with the previous clash analysis. The initial adaptive change analysis system, implemented on a laptop, required several hours to complete a clash-analysis task, which was previously accomplished in 2 weeks by large mainframes in a grid configuration.

The full system, capable of complex clash analysis, including electric, magnetic, stressing and other aspects of wing design, would further reduce effort and time required for eliminating consequences of design changes.

The obvious economic improvements in design change management, which were achieved in this project, stem from the fundamentally new principle on which the system was constructed, namely distributed decision-making in real time (as design changes were made) based on agent negotiation, rather than extensive batch-mode computation.

The ingenious relation between wing parts, "next to", or "neighbour", introduced into ontology enabled only potentially affected parts to be checked.

Adaptive design change management as developed for aircraft wing is, of course, applicable to the design of other engineering systems.

The same principles may be extended to the design of complex engineering systems with a view to trigger self-organisation whenever a disruptive event occurs. We may soon have an adaptive car, which autonomously modifies its configuration to accommodate changes in road conditions.

12

Adaptive scheduling of supply networks

The Problem

LEGO is known worldwide for its famous LEGO bricks. In addition to supplying over 50,000 retailers worldwide, LEGO also has about 100 own branded retail outlets, which provide the LEGO brand experience. As this retail operation is built to provide a unique shopping experience for consumers, lost sales and service level are considered of paramount importance.

Since the conception of the LEGO Brand Retail (LBR) outlets, the process of ordering stock to the retail outlets has been managed by the LEGO System, the organisational unit that purchases stock from the sole supplier. To create orders, the LBR inventory management team uses an in-house developed visual basic/Excel tool which is loaded with point-of-sales data summaries for the past 4 weeks of sale, inventory position and buying budget for each store. Based on this the LBR inventory management team creates orders for each outlet for each stock keeping unit (SKU), which are submitted to LEGO System.

As the moulding process of LEGO bricks is of very high quality, constraints on the lead time of moulds for special plastic bricks propagate into product packaging and subsequently provide constraints on supply. As some products are more popular than others LEGO System has to make a decision on how to allocate the stock amongst its retail customers, and this also determines how large or small will be a share of LBR.

LBR does not revise orders after the stocks have been allocated to them, as the allocation is forwarded automatically to LEGO Systems for picking, packing and dispatching. What determines the stock allocation is the sequence in which LEGO ERP system (a SAP ECC 6.0) receives the orders from LBR. The common procedure is that the orders of "the most important outlets" are processed early in the week, and "the less important outlets" later; therefore, the queue by which stock is assigned generates the self-fulfilling prophecy that well-performing outlets always will perform well as they are assigned stock early, whilst poorer performing outlets are assigned stock later.

What makes the problem worse is that the queue of orders is not being processed until weekend whereby the outlets which were assigned stock first have longer time lag from the latest demand signal, than those outlets whose orders are processed just before weekend processing.

LBR Outlets have different inbound capacity, so some of the products may be "in transit" after dispatch until all have been received by the outlets. This process of delaying goods receipt requires the carrier to store the goods until the outlet can receive all of it. However, as the pallets are packed to the convenience of the warehouse and not to the need of the outlet, the outlet manager has to evaluate and inspect which pallets are needed and subsequently request redelivery of the rest of the stock. At some outlets, the pallets are broken down to lose cartons/outers at the nearest depot, so that stock can be delivered successively. As this operation requires more handling, it is more expensive and only used where no other option is available.

This storage is costly and accounts for ~12% of the distribution cost. If LEGO Systems warehouse operation would be flexible, so that only the receivable quantities would be dispatched on a day-to-day basis, for example, in a pallet network, this would not significantly increase the total logistic cost.

The constraints of supply, aggregated usage of point-of-sale information, transfer of unresolved problems to suppliers and usage of in-house developed spreadsheets to overcome workload are, by experience, typical for human centric processes. The positive perspective is that LBR is aware of them and know that change is required to deliver its promise to the consumers.

This defines the requirements for the solution:

- The system must be able to scale up (and down) with the size of the business as it evolves with time.
- The system must be capable of dealing with 100+ outlets, thousands of SKUs and weekly, monthly and annual fluctuations in demand, including merger of belief-based long-term forecast with data-driven short-term forecasting.
- The system must be able to optimally exploit any given moment in assigning the limit supply of stock to outlets, so that lost sales are minimised, and service level and profit are maximised.
- The system must propose replenishment orders automatically and respond to any change in data. This is to be both interactive and to move away from batch processing of information, which is considered an inhibitor of transparency of the business.
- The system must allow users to override its decisions when required. However whenever users override the system they must be informed of the consequences to the rest of the business.

As LBR has no experience with this type of systems the leadership team decided to initiate a pilot project under the management of an internal researcher. The pilot project revealed additional problems. LBR and LEGO Systems usage of enterprise-wide applications are batch-based, which means that the transition to real-time information processing is a large development step. Other alternatives, such as SAP Forecasting and Replenishment (F&R) was evaluated, but due to SAP F&R's architecture, which generates orders under the assumption that the supplier has infinite capability to respond, the orders which SAP F&R creates are not revised after it has been decided how much stock is available, whereby the problem persists. In addition SAP F&R is based on batch information processing, which inhibits learning, as all interactions require a batch run before the user may learn the consequences of his/her actions.

To minimise the risks in the development process a stand-alone proof-of-concept model was developed over 6 months (described in the following section), with outlook for full-scale ERP integration in the following 6 months.

The Solution

Brief Overview

Complexity of a supply-chain process is caused mainly by uncertainty of demand and very limited storage space in retail outlets, combined with the relatively long period of time needed to complete the activities such as production, transportation, warehousing and distribution, which are required to replenish sold items in retail outlets.

Our solution is a multi-agent scheduler designed to refine demand forecasts and to rapidly react whenever forecasted demand does not materialises or an unexpected demand arrives [25]. Supply-chain schedule is created through a set of negotiations: Consumption agent negotiates with replenishment agents on how to ensure that the given retail outlet is never without stock and never overstocked; replenishment agent negotiate with product agents and transportation agents on how to deliver stock to the retail outlet minimising costs and getting correct timing; etc.

Knowledge Base

Ontology contains an XML-based construct of "how the supply-chain world works". Visual representation of ontology for LEGO supply-chain network is given in Fig. 35.

Virtual World

The whole processing of the initial scene and each individual event is performed by a community of agents called the virtual world. Each event represents a set of

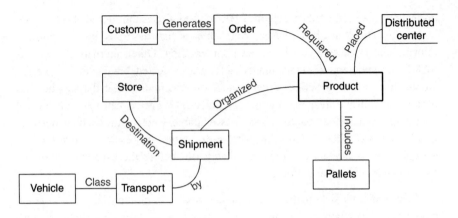

Figure 35: A fragment of supply-chain ontology.

changes happened in real world and triggers the activity of agents associated with the changed objects. The deviation from the stable result provoked by the changes is virtual world and the propagating changes in the scene. In this way the system reacts adaptively and in real time while maintaining the optimal KPIs.

Virtual world consists of several types of agents:

Consumption agent

Replenishment (delivery) agent

Stock agent

Product agent

Site (location) agent

Transportation agent

Consumption agent is a demand in the supply-and-demand network and responsible for making the consumption of a specific product at a specific moment of time possible. It can represent a forecasted consumption or a consumption that has really happened. The consumption demand is fully satisfied if there is enough stock for it at the scheduled time of consumption. If there is not enough stock, the consumption demand negotiates with replenishment agents to deliver more product items by this time.

Replenishment agent is also a demand and represents the delivery of products to a location. Replenishment agent negotiates with the transportation agent, product agent and site agent to get the restrictions and cost of delivery for a specific volume of products. Replenishment agents charge consumption agents for putting the products into the delivery and for changing the time of delivery. Replenishment agents produce additional stock levels. Stock agent represents the main resource in the swarm. The stock agents charge consumption demands for keeping product items in stock and provide information on the availability. If the stock level changes unexpectedly the stock agent pushes the product agent to reconsider the forecast.

Table 9: Examples of Object Classes, Relations, Attributes and Rules.

CLASS	RELATIONS	ATTRIBUTES	RULES
Customer (1)	Revenue (2) Product (3)	Customer type {unknown, club member}	Pays for products. Gets refund when returns product. Probably will select alternative product if wanted SKU is not there
Revenue (2)	Customer (1) Product (3)	Currency {GBP, USD, EUR, …}	Created when paid
Product (3)	Customer (1) Shelf (5) Store Order (7) Distribution Centre (8) Store Delivery (10) Shipment (11) DC order (14) Box (16)	Product id Height Width Length Price FMC value Theme Barcode	Must be packed into a box before shipping

Product agent is mainly responsible for maintaining the forecast of consumptions up-to-date. It knows the specifics of the product and changes the forecasted consumptions if the situation changes (e.g., if they are sold faster).

Site agent is responsible for tracking site restrictions (storage size, delivery processing power) and knows the cost of storage.

Transportation agent knows the limitations of a specific transportation channel (number of pallets) and cost function.

The solution supports the following list of events:

Expected occurrence of consumption

Unexpected occurrence of consumption

Non-occurrence of expected consumption

Change in consumption quantity

Unexpected change in stock level

An occurrence of replenishment

Change in current time

Any event can produce a chain of negotiations inside the virtual world. The length of the chain depends very much on the situation and can lead to a complete rescheduling in the worst case. Sometimes several events are processed at once. The possible negotiation relations and protocols between agents are presented in Fig. 36.

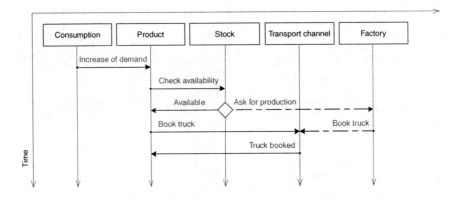

Figure 36: Basic protocols of agents negotiations.

The processing of events can affect time of delivery, allocation of consumptions to replenishments, consolidations of products in deliveries, size of consumptions, size of deliveries, cost of product storage and transportation, and/or company profit.

Logic of forecasting mechanism is presented in Fig. 37. The main idea here is that each new sale can trigger rescheduling of delivery with the goal to support service level or make more profit.

Though the final scheduler will contain all the conceptual elements, the proof-of-concept included only essential elements for the autonomous forecasting and scheduling, which could be managed in a single swarm governing deliveries and orders as a resource–demand network.

This permits incremental import of each event, which triggers adapted forecasting and repeated rescheduling following a plan/commit/execute protocol, which reflects the flexibility of real-world conditions. For example if a delivery has been planned, it may be changed until such point in time where it is necessary to commit the orders to the warehouse operation for picking, packing and subsequent dispatch, or for example a truck has to be booked a day in advance of the warehouse operation (Fig. 38).

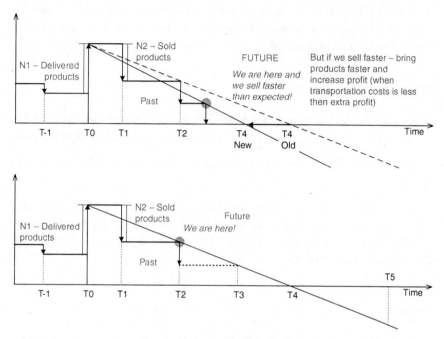

Figure 37:   Example of forecast recalculations.

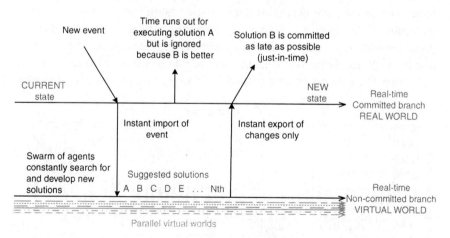

Figure 38:   Illustration of the incremental adaptive rescheduling as events are imported.

The scheduling process is based on two steps for every event. First the event signals that a product has been consumed, through point-of-sales records. This triggers a revision of the forecast for that particular product, based on the virtual world's current state, containing attributes such as current inventory level, current rate of sale and stochastic variation. The computation may show that an agent should be initialised to coordinate the delivery of a product. The "negotiation power" is determined by the agent profitability based on a trade-off between value of a lost sale and profit of a sale at the point in time when the product is expected to be sold.

Scheduler Architecture

To replicate the environment in which data is to be transformed into allocation and order decisions the standard architecture was used on the Microsoft .Net platform.

The "Real World" is captured in a Microsoft SQL server 2008 R2, with import through.

The "Data" is imported to the multi-agent virtual world by "day-end" with all point-of-sale records (location, material sold, quantity, etc.). The architecture permits that the data from the point-of-sales database could be forwarded to the MAS in real time, if needed.

Results

As the results were produced using the point-of-sales data (to represent the demand signal) the key decision was to apply LBRs existing processes (i.e., current practice) once more on the same data. This does not give the full picture but provides an indication of the effect of relaxing the constraints, which the business faces at present on real data (Fig. 39). In addition profit (of potential based on the assumption that the POS data is the real demand) was calculated for the relaxation of each constraint. The constraints were relaxed as follows, starting from the ideal case,

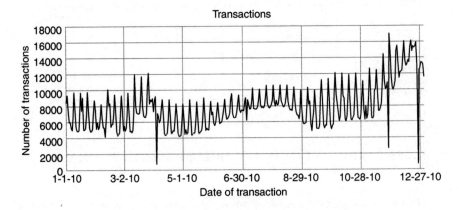

Figure 39: Example of real sales data from outlets.

Table 10: Results Achieved by the Prototype Scheduler.

SCENARIO	PROFIT (%)	SERVICE LEVEL (%)	LOST REVENUE (%)	COST (%)	ROW NUMBER
Theoretical ideal	100	100	0	100	1
(A1) Real-time scheduling with flexible business processes + "perfect forecast"	88	90	10	102	2
(A2) Real-time scheduling with flexible business processes + stochastic forecasting	81	86	16	105	3
(A3) Real-time scheduling with flexible business processes + trendline-based forecasting	76	86	20	105	4
(B1) Real-time scheduling with fixed business processes + "perfect forecast"	82	83	17	96	5
(B2) Real-time scheduling with fixed business processes + stochastic forecasting	76	79	22	96	6
(B3) Real-time scheduling with fixed business processes + trendline based forecasting	61	71	35	96	7
(C1) Fixed scheduling scheme and rigid business processes + "perfect forecast"	81	82	17	96	8
(C2) Fixed scheduling scheme & rigid business processes + stochastic forecasting	66	69	31	95	9
(C3) Fixed scheduling scheme and rigid business processes + trendline-based forecasting	56	66	40	95	10

and then added layers of constraints to match current practice. The combinations were:

A. Real-time scheduling with flexible business processes (idealistic future)

B. Real-time scheduling with fixed business processes (realistic future)

C. Fixed scheduling scheme and rigid business processes (current practice)

We have also considered the following different mechanisms of forecasts:

1. Perfect forecast – demand is precisely known in advance.

2. Stochastic forecasting – we know history and adaptively change probabilities of next sales.

3. Trendline-based forecasting (current practice).

The results are summarised in Table 10. The 10th row (bottom) indicates current practice, which is contrasted with the 3rd row that indicates an achievable state with real-time scheduling. Using the designed multi-agent solutions for selected US-based 20 outlets for 1-year trial period time LEGO has achieved the following results:

- Reduction of lost sale from 40% to 16%
- Increase in service level from 66% to 86%
- Increase in profitability from 56% to 81%

The achieved results are exceptionally positive and show the value of a full-scale LEGO supply-chain multi-agent solution, which will be able to dynamically and adaptively reschedule not only outlets transportation deliveries but also manufacturing and managing cross-docks inbound and outbound in real time.

The results of first stage of developments using our multi-agent platform and technology are showing many benefits for supply chains including openness to new events, high flexibility and adaptability, performance and reliability.

Future improvements include the following: support product life cycle, removing non-selling products, merger with belief-based forecast realised deliveries and some others.

Next step will be focused on integrating LBR with the existing SAP system.

13

Adaptive scheduling of services for the international space station

The Problem

Servicing of the International Space Station (ISS) is a complex process consisting of many interrelated tasks, including scheduling of space flights (with distinct phases of starts, dockings and undockings); managing piloted (manned) spaceships; supporting space crew life activity and delivering to the space station of laboratory equipment, various materials and instruments. Servicing is carried out under conditions of severe space, weight and time constraints and frequent occurrences of disruptive events.

All this work was, until recently, done manually by a large number of scientists, engineers and managers, who had to make millions of iterations and interaction to come to a compromise solution.

ISS support can be partitioned into the following tasks:

- Flight program design, which produces a schedule of dockings of spaceships to ISS modules (segments), considering a variety of constraints, i.e., minimal period of time between operations of docking and undocking; permanent presence of at least one piloted ship docked to the station and different preferences for docking of different ship types.
- Strategic and operational scheduling of cargo flow, which produces a plan of deliveries of units, blocks and systems for cargo flights and piloted (manned) spaceships, based on the flight program.
- Strategic and tactical scheduling of fuel deliveries and consumption, based on a forecast on ISS position changes, the solar activity, operations plan and the flight program.
- Scheduling of deliveries of water, food and other human life activity support items, based on information about expeditions and the flight program.
- Scheduling of cargo returns from the station.
- Scheduling of flight crew.

Scheduling of flights, cargo flow and resources for ISS has several stages with different scheduling horizons. First, there is a need to create a strategic model of cargo flow, which helps to calculate the number of required transportation flights per year on the basis of the number of expected expeditions. Then starts the interactive design of the flight program. At this stage there is a need to achieve an agreement between all involved parties on the number and times of dockings and undockings of spaceships to ISS modules, considering time frames of possible starts of spaceships, the solar activity, configuration and expected position of ISS, space crew requirements, etc. Several versions of the flight program are created and examined at this stage before the final plan is signed and published.

After the flight program has been agreed the concurrent work starts on scheduling of cargo flow, fuel and water. Cargo volumes are distributed between transportation space flights and manned flights (when special assistance is required) on the basis of data on average daily consumption. The number of astronauts and information about dates of starts and dockings are taken from the signed-off flight program. Fuel and water deliveries are calculated on the basis of data about the ISS position corrections and consumption for docking and other space operations. Cargo flow plan is then expanded to take into account the load that needs to be returned from the ISS back to earth.

The main scheduling problem here is the interdependence of all decisions, which requires precise coordination. The capacity of spaceships is limited and when an unpredictable demand for additional cargo arrives, fuel or water volumes may need to be reduced, and vice versa.

The Solution

Brief Overview

The solution, designed for supporting the ISS, is a unique *network of adaptive multi-agent schedulers, which itself is adaptive.* Constituent schedulers cooperate or compete with each other depending on context. Constituent agents in each scheduler, assigned to individual demands and resources, are also designed to cooperate or compete with each other [42].

The following constituent schedulers have been implemented:

- Adaptive scheduler for flight program design
- Adaptive scheduler for cargo flow
- Adaptive scheduler for fuel and water deliveries
- Adaptive scheduler for returns and utilisation
- Adaptive scheduler for flight crew

Additional schedulers can be developed, when required, and easily connected into the overall network of schedulers.

Individual agents, schedulers and the whole network provide services to users at the appropriate levels, reacting in real time to every new demand, disruption in services or change in resources.

Schedulers that are built on a recently developed multi-agent platform are briefly described in Chapter 3.

Knowledge Base

All ISS servicing domain knowledge is captured in ontology and factual databases, which together represent the scheduling knowledge base. A fragment of ontology is represented in Fig. 40.

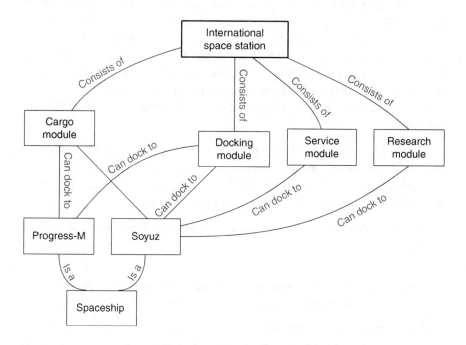

Figure 40: A fragment of flight program ontology.

Domain object classes represented in ontology include ISS, ISS module, flight, space, spaceship, crew, cargo, fuel, port, flight program, schedule. Object classes are connected by relations into a network, which can be modified by users with the help of a user interface that allows ontology to be edited without system shutdown. Users can introduce, if necessary, new types of spaceships and flights (and specify to what ports they should be docked); new types of ports/modules; and new types of cargo and operations. The user interface of the flight program and other editors will change correspondingly, providing new capabilities for interactive scheduling.

Ontology provides a basis for constructing instantaneous models of domain, known as scenes.

Virtual World

Virtual world of each scheduler has specialised types of agents. For example, flight-program Scheduler has spaceship agent, expedition agent and astronaut agent types, whilst cargo-flow scheduler has cargo agent and flight agent types. Some agent types exist in two or more virtual worlds. The rule is that every two virtual worlds should have agents of at least one common type, to facilitate interaction between schedulers.

For example, the flight agent is introduced into both flight-program scheduler and cargo-flow scheduler. If, due to a spaceship preparation delay, the start of a flight is postponed, the agent of this flight, resident in the flight-program virtual world, will change its plan, i.e., it will shift the dates of start, docking and undocking. Because it acts in both the flight-program and cargo-flow scene, its message about the changes will alert cargo agents in the cargo-flow scene to the delay of their flight and give them an opportunity to negotiate "jumping" into another flight, if necessary.

Conversely, if some cargoes are reduced, the utilisation of a flight can become too low, which will be represented in a cargo-flow scene by a partially satisfied or unsatisfied flight agent. This agent will try to shift its flight to a later time in the flight program to become more attractive for cargo agents.

Virtual worlds of the ISS servicing system are populated with three types of agents:

1. *Decision-maker agents,* representing those who participate in real-world negotiations: cargo managers, engineers and scientists, top management.

2. *Object agents* (that can still act as independent entities and have own objectives and constraints), representing spaceships, flights, expeditions, astronauts, cargo items, systems, fuel, water, etc.

3. *Group agents* (that negotiate on behalf of groups of the agents), representing flight-program options, cargo-flow schedules, fuel and water tactical calculations, etc.

Virtual world of each scheduler forms a separate swarm of agents, where agents of different types can communicate. Although each constituent agent of a swarm has its own preferences and constraints, it can interact with agents belonging to another swarm using preferences and constraints of the whole swarm.

Here is an example of a typical agent interaction.

- When a new request to allocate a cargo to a certain flight at a certain time arrives from a curator, a new cargo agent is created.
- The new cargo agent interacts with the spaceship agents that have flights in the relevant flight program, searching for an allocation opportunity. This interaction involves sending top-level messages between the cargo-flow scheduler and flight-program scheduler.
- Available options are prioritised taking into account cargo requirements and transaction values.
- If there is enough free space on a selected flight, and cargo fits in terms of weight and size, the new delivery is included into the schedule.
- Alternately, the following actions are performed:

  - Flight agent sends a request to fuel agent to reduce the volume of fuel delivered on this flight, taking into account the pre-defined amount of fuel that must be always available on ISS.
  - If the obtainable reduction of fuel is not sufficient, flight agent sends a message to water agent requesting water delivery reduction.
  - If fuel and water reductions are not sufficient, cargo agents are pushed to move their cargoes to other flights, if possible.

Two points here are of high importance:

1. Not all cargoes are independent. Two or more cargoes can be linked by being placed in the same box or in the same unit. In such a case before one cargo is moved to another flight, the system should consider interests of other linked cargoes as well as the profitability of the move.

2. When one or several cargoes move, they free some space that can be greater than it is required to allocate a new cargo. In such a case, it is necessary to initiate rescheduling of water and fuel. If fuel and/or water agents previously had to reduce fuel and/or water volumes, now they have an opportunity to restore them.

In the above negotiation process it is impossible to pre-define any sequence of steps or logic. Negotiation process is not an algorithm.

User Interfaces

An examples of user interfaces are shown in Fig. 41.

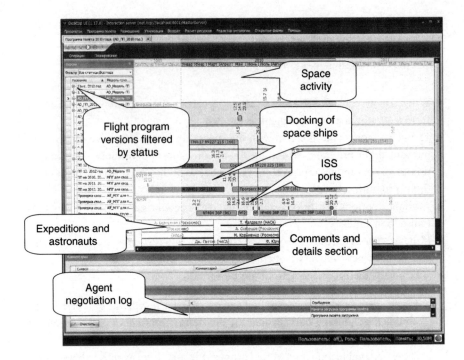

Figure 41: Flight program interactive design editor.

Results

The system was used to design several flight programs for a period 2010–2014 and to schedule cargo flows and resources for 2011. The system enabled the client to design and compare several options of flight programs, including possible reactions to unpredictable events. The key result is a reduction in time spent on scheduling and the consequent ability to simulate different schedule options and to support negotiations between the involved departments aimed at finding better reactions to external events. This particular feature helped to minimise possible risks and prepare the client better for managing unpredictable events.

Integration with inventory management system (using import and export files of specific format) allows updating schedules with actual data and initiating rescheduling in real time.

14

Adaptive scheduling of a fleet of satellites

The Problem

Space industry is experiencing a decisive paradigm shift. Big, heavy, expensive, multifunctional satellites are being replaced by swarms of small, light, cheap satellites, each performing a specialised service and capable of competing and cooperating with each other. New types of "pico" satellites are up to 1 kg in weight. Slightly larger units may go up to 10 kg.

There is an intriguing parallel between this bold step undertaken by space industry and our own approach of replacing big, expensive and rigid conventional software with swarms of small, agile, competing/cooperating software agents.

Our assertion is that this trend from big, rigid units to networks of small and flexible nodes is going to spread to most areas of business and engineering.

Our client was concerned with a network of Earth Observation Satellites engaged in tasks such as:

- Ecology monitoring
- Search for mobile objects, e.g., ships
- Monitoring of large hydro generating plants
- Prevention of fires
- Assessment of consequences of fires

Each satellite in the network had certain intelligent capabilities:

- Measurement of its own coordinates
- Analysis of observed situations
- Making decisions on further actions
- Making proposals to other satellites in the network
- Engaging in two-way interaction with other satellites and with the network control centre (sending and receiving messages)
- Conducting negotiations and coordinating decisions
- Transmitting data

Our task was to solve two problems: the analysis of observed situations (pattern recognition) and scheduling of satellite swarm activities.

Examples of disruptive events, which trigger rescheduling included arrival of a new task, completion of a task, satellite failure and launching of a new satellite.

The Solution

Brief Overview

Satellite swarms solve complex pattern recognition problems in a complex environment characterised by frequent occurrence of unpredictable disruptive events.

Our solution [43] consisted of two MAS, one for adaptive pattern recognition and the other for adaptive scheduling of satellite activities.

In the first version both systems were located at the earth control station. The intention is however to build a distributed scheduling and pattern recognition system, with its modules located on each satellite. This will make the earth control centre a surplus to requirements and will enable swarms of satellites to be self-sufficient. The idea is for clients to order an observation task, such as monitoring a house and garden during a holiday period, directly from the company website and the task to be passed to the satellite swarm, which would take care of scheduling of observations and return of observation results without any need to use earth control centre (Fig. 42)

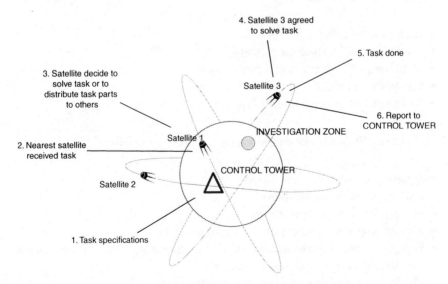

Figure 42:   Satellite swarm operation.

Knowledge Base

Our initial solution envisaged that both multi-agent systems are served by one common ontology, which contained the following classes of objects: observation target, town, house, road, pipeline, forest, tree, danger, high-temperature spot, radiation spot, satellite, task, control centre, as shown in Fig. 43.

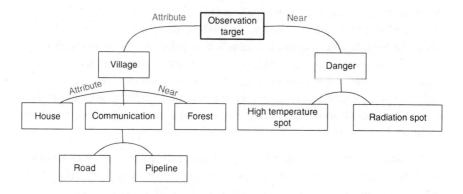

Figure 43: A fragment of satellite observation and scheduling ontology.

Virtual Worlds

Our solution envisaged two virtual worlds, one for pattern recognition and the other for scheduling.

Virtual World of Pattern Recognition

Virtual world of pattern recognition is populated by types of agents such as observation target agent, building agent, road agent and fire agent. Types of agents depend upon the type of observations that are carried out by the swarm.

An observation target agent is assigned to a new observed situation picked up by a satellite. The observation target agent analyses the situation and engages relevant specialised agents such as building agent, road agent and fire agent, to search for buildings, roads and fires, respectively. Thus, pattern recognition is done in distributed manner by a swarm of agents each specialising in detecting specific objects (buildings, roads) or phenomena (fire) and then, with the help of the observation target agent, linking objects and activities together into observation results.

It is often necessary for several satellites to cooperate on a pattern recognition task. For example, to detect fires it is required to have specialised heat-detecting equipment, which is available on only a few satellites.

Virtual World of Scheduling
Virtual world of scheduling is populated by types of agents such as satellite agent, task agent and control centre agent (enterprise agent).

A task agent is assigned to a new task received by the scheduler from the control centre or from a satellite. The new task agent initiates the exchange of messages with satellite agents aimed at determining which satellite is the most suitable to undertake the new task. Negotiations usually proceed in waves: the new task is first offered to the nearest satellite, which decides if it can do the complete task, or only a part of the task, and passes the request to the next satellite, if necessary. It is quite common for satellites to cooperate on a task, each performing a part of which it is best suited. Satellite agents may elect a leader satellite agent to coordinate collaborative activities.

Criteria for arriving at the decision include satellite observation capabilities, location, availability and cost of observations. Negotiations may involve the enterprise agent, whose duty is to ensure that the specified enterprise value is maximised.

If a satellite fails, its agent sends messages to all affected members of the swarm and their agents reschedule the allocation of duties to tasks, accordingly.

Rescheduling is also required when control centre sends a request to undertake immediately a new urgent task, such as new fire detection.

Connecting Virtual and Real Worlds

Swarms of satellites have a number of established communication channels:

- Direct communication between satellites if they are in the line of vision and within specified distances
- The use of selected communication satellites on geo-static orbits
- Communication via earth control centre and data processing centre.

Results

Preliminary results show that adaptive pattern recognition and scheduling generate results of higher quality, faster and cheaper than previous arrangements. In addition the solution is scalable and very reliable. Real-time scheduling was particularly useful because of unpredictable demand and frequent disruptions of the planned service.

Fig. 44 shows how agent negotiations reduce observation time when the number of observation targets increases.

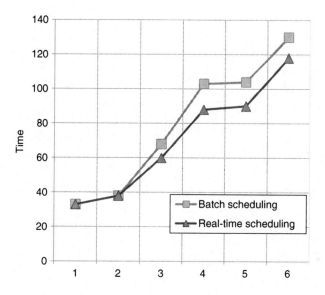

Figure 44: Advantage of real-time scheduling increases with the loading.

15

Adaptive scheduling of high-speed railways

The Problem

Railway scheduling problem can be formulated as the allocation of trains to blocks, where a block is a section of a railway line, which can be occupied only by one train. Standard conditions include:

- Different trains travel with different speeds.
- Different trains have different priorities.
- A train can overtake another train at a station or, if necessary, using a free block of the line normally reserved for trains travelling in the opposite direction.
- The capacity of a station to hold trains, which are being overtaken, is limited.

Train scheduling is subject to the occurrence of unpredictable disruptive events, including:

- Train failures
- Track failures
- Train delays
- Track repair delays

Whenever a disruptive event occurs, the schedule must be changed to accommodate the disruption with the minimal consequences to trains that are not directly affected.

Our task was to develop a system for scheduling of trains on a very busy railway mainline with the specific requirement that the direct high-speed trains are not allowed to be late whatever the track conditions may be. Track failures were frequent and repair works occasionally required up to 8 hours of track closures. The published train timetable produced by railway headquarters was given to us as a reference and a starting point for any scheduling.

The Solution

Brief Overview

An event driven multi-agent scheduler was developed [44] capable of (a) entering the official train timetable as the initial state of the system, (b) producing the schedule covering all constituent resources and (c) modifying the schedule, in real time, whenever a disruptive event occurred.

Modified schedules were sent to affected resources in real time enabling the train table to be dynamically adjusted in order to maintain a strict correspondence with the situation in the field.

Knowledge Base

Ontology contained objects such as train, station, sidetrack and block, linked by relations, such as "train occupies block", "train travels to station" and "sidetrack belongs to station". Each object was described by appropriate attributes.

Virtual World

Virtual world contained agent types such as train agent, station agent, sidetrack agent and block agent.

Scheduling is done by negotiation between demand agents and resource agents, where a typical demand agent is train agent and a typical resource agent is block agent. The basis for the negotiation is the premise that for a train to travel from A to B all blocks between these two points must be free from other trains at the time when the train is scheduled to reach them. When a train seeks a sidetrack at a station to wait to be overtaken by a higher priority train, resource agents involved in negotiation will be station agents and sidetrack agents (Fig. 45).

The schedule is constructed in several stages.

The first stage is production of a rough schedule for all trains based on the official timetable. The schedule is built for all trains in parallel exposing points of conflicts between trains (more than one train on a block), if any.

The second stage is concerned with the elimination of conflicts. Train agents and block agents negotiate which of the trains that are in conflict will enter the contested block first, respecting, whenever possible, specified train priorities. Whenever a train has to overtake another train, affected station agents and sidetrack agents get involved in negotiations.

The third stage irons out anomalies, such as excessive delays imposed on some of the low priority trains, aiming to produce a well-balanced schedule.

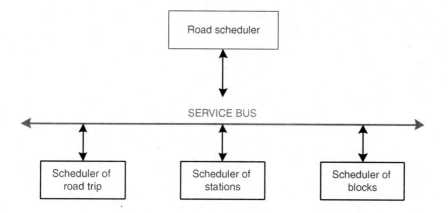

Figure 45: Scheduling of trains by a swarm of schedulers.

All negotiations are conducted with the aim of maximising enterprise value, which is a complex function that balances different, often conflicting, goals, i.e., respecting specified train priorities, minimising delays, minimising the use of blocks of the line reserved for trains travelling in opposite direction and special train constrains. In the third stage attempts to increase enterprise value are carried out until the process reaches the point of diminishing returns.

If the selected scheduling strategy does not lead to the satisfactory enterprise value, agents may autonomously decide to destroy the inadequate schedule and start the process from scratch, following alternative strategies (constructive destruction). The same may happen if the user of the system (a dispatcher) decides that the schedule produced by agents is inadequate.

Connecting Virtual and Real Worlds

The scheduler receives inputs from and sends outputs to the railways information processing system.

Results

The prototype adaptive multi-agent scheduler has demonstrated that it can substantially reduce time required to reschedule affected trains after the occurrence of a disruptive event and improve the utilisation of railway resources. At the time of writing the project was in an initial stage.

16

Adaptive scheduling of manufacturing

The Problem

In general, manufacturing problem can be formulated as the allocation of manu-facturing resources (e.g., plants, machine tools, transportation, storage, materials, parts and human operators) to orders in space and time, under conditions of frequent occurrence of unpredictable disruptive events (e.g., changes of orders, failures of resources, delays, human errors) – a typical modern logistic problem.

Let us consider two case studies, Client 1 – manufacturing of electronic devices and Client 2 – manufacturing and repair of aircraft jet engines.

Electronic instrument manufacturer is a very large industrial organisation with multiple manufacturing units, which initially ordered from us a scheduler for one workshop handling 30–40 orders per day for products with 20–30 components and 15–20 manufacturing operations per product. The workshop employs 120 operators on a regular basis.

Jet engine manufacturer and repairer has 40 workshops and 4,000 workers, handles 1,000 orders per day, and has more than 1,000 suppliers. Production plans for different workshops are interdependent and have to satisfy many interlinked constraints. Products are complicated and subject to continuous innovation and improvement. Machine tools are sophisticated and include multi-purpose robots and sensors. Manufacturing is supported by legacy systems. Our initial order was for a scheduler for one workshop.

The Solution

Brief Overview

Two adaptive multi-agent schedulers have been developed [45,46], one for each client, based on our standard architecture described in Part 1. The schedulers react rapidly to disruptive events and attempt to increase the enterprise value by improving the allocation of resources to orders, whenever there is a slack period between two successive disruptive events. The schedulers are designed to work interactively with dispatchers allowing them to change the schedule constructed by agents.

Knowledge Base

Ontology for both systems contains classes of objects such as order, workshop, operator, machine tool, process, operation and product. Examples of attributes are for order – value, priority, deadline and details; for operator – skills, wages, schedule and performance.

Ontology for each client is customised to include polices, rules and regulations on scheduling, specific to the client.

Virtual World

Virtual worlds of both schedulers are populated by agents such as order agent, enterprise agent, operator agent, machine tool agent, process agent, operation agent and product agent. Examples of agent tasks are for order agent – to get the best possible resources; for enterprise agent – to maximise enterprise value by a variety of means, e.g., by adjusting scheduling strategy, by constructive destruction of a schedule or by adjusting virtual money supply to agents; for operator agent – to get the schedule, which will ensure the best wages or, which will ensure tasks that will enhance experience.

Agent behaviour during negotiations is different for different clients reflecting differences in manufacturing resources and operations, and in manufacturing practices.

The assignment of operations to machine tools very often involves the need for resolving conflicts caused when a new operation wants to occupy the time slot already occupied by other operations. A conflict is usually eliminated by a sequence of negotiations attempting to move previously allocated operations forward or back in time to accommodate the new operation. The process of resolving a conflict by negotiation is illustrated by Figs. 46–48.

Various categories of users are provided with interfaces designed for their requirements. For example, the screen showing event queues enable managers to input a new event (e.g., a new urgent order) and initiate rescheduling to accommodate that event, whilst the screen showing interdependences of manufacturing

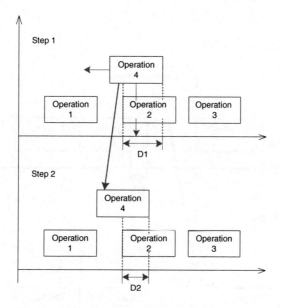

Figure 46: Operation 4 cannot fit between operations 1 and 2, moving it forward
in time helps but it is still not sufficient.

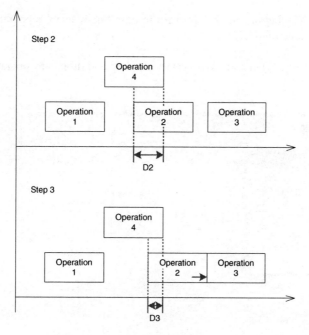

Figure 47: Moving operation 2 back in time helps but it is still not sufficient.

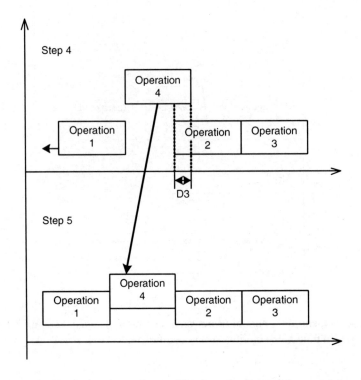

Figure 48: Moving operation 1 forward in time finally enables operation 4 to be accommodated.

operations (Fig. 49) enables supervisors to "drag and drop" any operation on any operator.

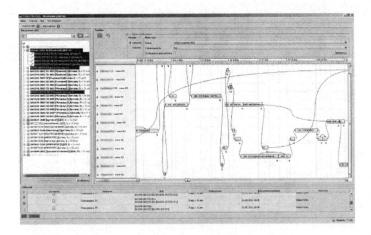

Figure 49: Interactive screen showing interdependencies of manufacturing operations.

Connecting Virtual and Real Worlds

The schedulers are linked to the clients' information processing systems via databases from which they read inputs, when triggered, and into which they write real-time outputs.

Results

The scheduler for Client 1 was developed in 9 months and is now in regular operation. It is in a daily use by about 30 users, including workshop managers, dispatchers, technologists and supervisors.

According to top management of the Client 1, the main contribution of the scheduler is that it:

- Provided full transparency of the manufacturing planning process
- Maintains a clear picture of the use of manufacturing resources
- Enables managers to foresee manufacturing bottlenecks
- Reacts rapidly and positively to disruptions

In addition, the scheduler:

- Speeded up the transition from paper-based to electronic handling of documents in the whole host workshop
- Increased productivity of the manufacturing unit by fully autonomous and high-quality scheduling
- Simplified manufacturing management tasks by producing timely and accurate manufacturing documentation and instructions for operators
- Enabled managers to interactively intervene and modify tasks or schedules, if required

The scheduler is linked with the factory ERP system and provides information required to calculate operators' wages on "fact versus plan" basis.

A link with the client's CAD/CAM (computer-aided design/computer-aided manufacturing) system provides the scheduler with electronic description of products and manufacturing operations.

The second project, for Client 2, is in an early stage. Provisional results have demonstrated capabilities of adaptive scheduling to considerably improve the effectiveness of manufacturing and the client has agreed to extend the project to cover other workshops.

17

Adaptive management of service teams

The Problem

Our client operated a large network of technicians working in small teams servicing gas installations. Visits to customers were scheduled by trained dispatchers who received calls from customers, which were mostly demands for urgent interventions. Dispatchers were overworked and were concerned only with meeting individual demands without having an overall picture of requirements. There was no attempt to coordinate servicing work. The number of demands was much greater than the available resources.

Plans were frequently disrupted by events such as unexpected urgent demand, cancellation of a demand, transport failure and delay in completing a task.

The client required a scheduler capable of reducing:

- Time required to schedule servicing tasks
- Overall travelling time of service teams
- Time required to complete servicing tasks

In other words, the client required a scheduler capable of increasing productivity of servicing teams.

The Solution

Brief Overview

An adaptive multi-agent scheduler was developed capable of allocating tasks to servicing teams in real time, which was made available to clients managing servicing teams in three versions [48]:

1. Under license – the standard scheduler is installed on a stand-alone server; users access the scheduler using passwords over a local network or the Internet.

2. Customised scheduler – the scheduler is modified to meet every single requirement of the client and is sold as one-off product.

3. Scheduling as a service – clients pay subscription fees for accessing the scheduler when required.

A diagram showing how the system works in shown in Fig. 50.

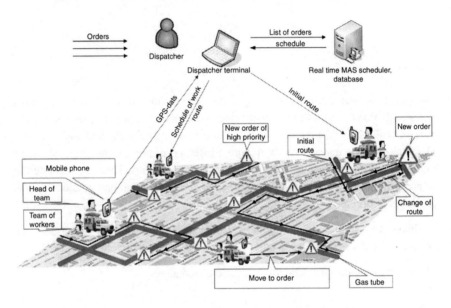

Figure 50:   Adaptive scheduling of servicing teams.

Knowledge Base

Examples of key object classes stored in ontology are task, servicing team, shift, transport and route. Examples of attributes are, for task, location, importance, duration and specification; and for servicing team number of members, capabilities, duration and state.

A scene is an instantaneous model of the business showing which servicing team is working on which task. A scene is changing with every disruptive event. Logs of scenes are preserved for analysis.

Virtual World

Virtual world is populated with agents. Examples of the most important agents are:

Task agent, whose objective is to search for a servicing team able to start work and complete it as soon as possible, at the appropriate quality.

Shift agent, whose objective is to minimise travelling time between two consecutive tasks and to complete as many tasks as practical during a shift.

Team agent, whose objective is to get the tasks that will maximise team productivity.

All decisions are made as a result of negotiations between appropriate agents.

Connecting Virtual and Real Worlds

All demands for servicing are received by telephone and registering into the scheduler by dispatchers. Schedules are sent to servicing team mobiles by texts. Reports by servicing teams are sent from their mobiles by texts directly to the scheduler.

Results

The scheduler is implemented and used for mission critical functions achieving 40% increase in productivity of mobile teams. Each team of service engineers has managed to complete, on average, 12 tasks a day instead of 7.

In addition, the scheduler enables managers to have, at any given moment, a clear picture of the overall operation of service teams depicted on a map, as well as detailed information on important aspects of the business, such as which team is working on which task at which location; the current progress of task fulfilment for each team; the number of calls for servicing yet to be allocated; current productivity of each individual service technician, each service team and the enterprise as a whole and unit costs of every servicing operation.

The scheduler has won a "product of the year" award at the international exhibition Soft-Tool 2011.

18

Adaptive project management

The Problem

The key difference between business management and project management is that a project has a specified beginning and an end. The essence is the same: the allocation of resources (human, physical, financial and intellectual) to demands with the aim to maximise specified value.

Standard challenges are high competition for resources, stringent deadlines and frequent unpredictable disruptive events.

General obstacles to successful accomplishment of a project include:

- Functional organisation, which inevitably impedes interdepartmental cooperation.
- Bureaucratic management, which is more concerned with lines of command and reporting than with the full use of project member's initiative and creativity and which negatively affects their motivation.
- Fixed term, as opposed to real-time project planning, which leads to a rapid divergence between the project plan and reality.

Large enterprises commonly operate several projects concurrently. What is best for an individual project it is not always best for the enterprise and therefore it is necessary to implement coordination of concurrently run projects with the objective of maximising enterprise value.

Our client was one of the key space technology organisations, which operates, at any time, many concurrent mission critical projects.

The Solution

Brief Overview

The adaptive project management system was developed to allocate project resources (human, physical and intellectual) to project tasks [49]. It is envisaged that several project management systems will operate concurrently, each by a swarm of agents, and that these swarms will cooperate with each other to ensure that enterprise value is maximised.

Knowledge Base

Examples of classes of objects in ontology are enterprise, organisational unit, project, task, project member (human resource), physical resource, document, software resource and process.

Examples of attributes are, for task, content, cost, duration, deadline and preferences; and for project member, organisational unit, competences, profile, schedule, current task, salary, achievements and preferences.

A fragment of enterprise ontology is shown in Fig. 51.

Virtual World

Examples of agents that populate the virtual world include:

Task agent, whose objective is to search for the best resources capable of meeting its requirements.

Human resource agent, whose objective is to get the best possible task, which will keep the project participant fully occupied, provide opportunities for bonuses and/or enable the participant to learn new skills or get new experience.

Physical resource agent, whose objective is to maximise resource utilisation.

Project agent, whose objective is to maximise project value.

Enterprise agent, whose objective is to maximise enterprise value.

All decisions are made through agent negotiations, as exemplified by the following process: task agents send messages to human resource agents with required competences inviting them to contribute to task fulfilments. Human resource agents that are available send their bids. Task agents offer project participation to agents that sent the best bids.

When a new task arrives a new task agent is created. The new task agent consults ontology to find out what are its objectives and how to achieve them, and proceeds to send messages to selected human resource agents inviting them to bid for project participation. It is very likely that this invitation will result in rescheduling, giving an opportunity to human resource agents that were not fully satisfied with their previous allocations to improve their positions. Remuneration, including bonuses,

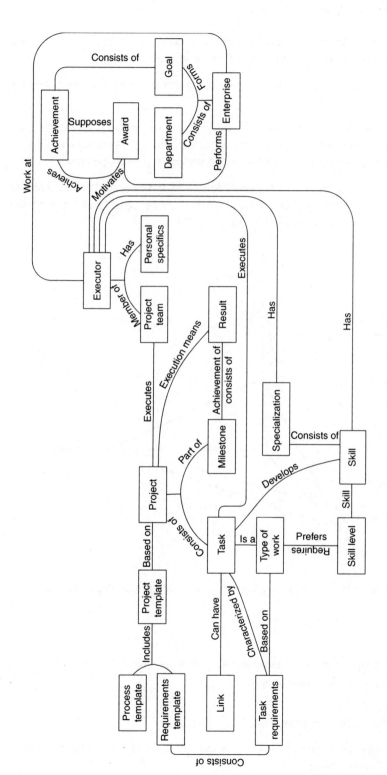

Figure 51: A fragment of enterprise ontology.

if any, is calculated on the basis of project members' participation and achieved results. Enterprise members may participate in several projects.

The allocation of physical and software resources is done in an analogous manner.

Almost all features discussed in Chapter 3 have been employed to maximise effectiveness of agent negotiation, such as virtual microeconomics, agent satisfaction, agent proactivity, enterprise agents and swarm cooperation.

Decisions on allocation of resources to project tasks are made using multiple criteria, e.g., minimising completion time, maximising quality and minimising identified risks, as illustrated in Fig. 52.

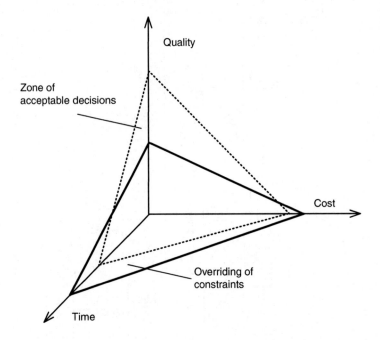

Figure 52: Decisions on allocation are made using multiple criteria.

Results

The first adaptive project management system was recently implemented and tested achieving the following results:

10–15% increase in project member productivity

3–4 times reduction in manpower required for project scheduling, monitoring and coordination

2–3 times reduction of response time to unpredictable disruptive events

15–30% increase in the number of projects completion on budget and in time

A significant increase in project member motivation

A possibility to increase the number of projects operating in parallel without increasing the number of employees

Further work includes implementing several project management systems and ensuring that they cooperate with each other.

PART 3

A roadmap into the future

19

A vision and ideas

A Shift from Personal to Business Applications

In the late 20th and early 21st centuries we have witnessed a surge of developments in IT *for personal use*, as exemplified by mobile phones, smart phones, tablets, wearable devices, the integration of the Internet and smart television by means of devices such as Apple TV, voice-over-the-Internet applications such as Skype, social networks such as Facebook, YouTube, Blog and Twitter, the Internet search engines such as Google, and many applications for exchanging, downloading and storing of photos and music.

In a short period of time the new IT transformed our society and changed the way we communicate with each other and form communities of interests. It is astonishing that nearly a half of all people who live on this planet are now using the Internet.

Apple emerged as the most influential company in the world because it successfully predicted the focus on consumers and developed appropriate products.

But what is going to happen in the rest of the 21st century?

Our prediction is that the focus of IT innovations will shift from personal to commercial, administrative and engineering applications.

The driving force will be the relentless increase in the complexity of the Internet-based global market. The number of businesses, which uses the Internet to sell or buy goods, to invest or acquires capital and, in particular, to sell and buy knowledge-based services, will continue growing.

As a result, the size and dynamics of the global market will push unpredictability of demand and supply to the level at which more and more businesses and administrations will discover that it is essential to learn how to manage complexity and become adaptive.

So what will be the major focus of innovations in the near future?

Most probably, *the Internet of Things (IoT), Digital Enterprise, Smart City and Smart Logistics.*

And which company will emerge as the most influential and replace Apple in the pole position?

Well, let's not speculate, one thing is only sure, it will be the company that has by now understood the new direction and focused on products and services for the IoT, digital enterprise, smart city and smart logistics.

Let us consider some of ideas how to develop further our systems for adaptive allocation of resources to demands in order to fit into the Vision outlined above.

The IoT

The intention is to connect to the Internet, by means of electronic tags, all physical objects that are useful for business and personal use: transportation resources such as cars, trucks, trains, railway carriages, tractors, ships, airplanes, helicopters, conveyers, carts, factories, plants, shop floors, machine-tools, robots, warehouses, shelves, retail outlets, products, goods, assemblies, components, pallets and packages and home appliances.

Once connected to the Internet, the "things" can start communicating with each other without the involvement of humans.

- A parcel may ask a warehouse robot to load it on the truck travelling to its destination.
- A car on a motorway may ask the car in front for permission to be electronically locked together in a car–train.
- An airliner may ask another aircraft to change flight direction to avoid a near miss.
- A truck may broadcast to servicing garages along his route that it has a puncture and needs a new tyre, garages that are willing to replace the tyre will submit bids, the truck will consider bids and select the best offer for tyre replacement.

In time, simple electronic tags attached to things will be replaced with processors with resident agents, which will negotiate with agents resident on web-services containing demands, how to allocate things to demands. The negotiation process will be conducted, of course, in real time.

By 2020 the number of Internet-connected things is expected to reach 30 billions, each with a unique IP address.

After the first surge in the development of devices for connecting things to the Internet there will be a disappointment with software for managing the usage of the connected resources. We shall be ready with a variety of systems for adaptive allocation of things, as resources for business or personal use, to demands. Our IoT ideas are described in the following under relevant application titles.

Digital Enterprise

As complexity of the Internet-based global market increases further, organisations will start developing adaptive business processes and gain competitive edge by extracting knowledge from accumulated data and text. New organisations will emerge designed from scratch as digital enterprises, with possibly all information processing activities centred on enterprise knowledge base with enterprise ontology in its core.

Digital enterprise may replace corporation as the main business model. This switch is fundamental – digital enterprises generate substantial value added by outsourcing processing of materials and goods and keeping all data and information processing in the cloud. The core activity of a digital enterprise is intellectual work.

The concept of digital enterprise is of course new and imprecisely defined. Our view is that its key attributes will include at least some of those listed below and we shall be ready to deliver supporting systems.

Adaptability and Innovation

Allocation of resources (human, physical, financial and intellectual) will be performed in real time, driven by the occurrence of disruptive events. Adaptive strategy, as outlined in Chapter 2, will be in place. Business processes will be designed to be adaptive. The possible drift into failure due to frequent adaptations will be arrested and reversed by spontaneous innovation.

Online Access to Resources

Human, physical, financial and intellectual (knowledge) resources will be accessible online by authorised users whatever their location (office, home, travel) or access tool (desktops, laptops, tablets, smart phones).

Adaptive Websites

Every visitor to a website has own interests and requirements and yet they all have to deal with the same standard content presentation. We have prototyped a site, which will get into conversation with each visitor and adapt the site to visitor's preferences. Here is briefly how it works: A personal agent is assigned to the visitor, which ascertains if the visitor has preferences by engaging him/her in written conversation in a language of visitor's choice. Personal agent then consults site ontology to establish what to do and negotiates with content agents how to rearrange site content presentation to meet visitor preferences. Returning visitors are given privileged status, which allows them to ask for information that is not available on the site but could be captured by personal agent and sent to them, say, by email.

IT as a Service

Data will be in the cloud and information processing tools will be developed or purchased as web-based services.

Distributed Organisation

Organisational structure will be a network of self-contained units, which compete and cooperate with each other. Business will self-organise to adapt to changing market conditions by changing connections and/or nodes of its organisational network.

Distributed Decision-Making

All stakeholders affected by a particular decision will be involved in decision-making.

Focus on Knowledge Discovery

IoT will increase pressure on data centres. As the Internet expands and we continue to digitise everything in our sight, we shall accumulate huge amount of information in digital form. The hottest topics in digital enterprise circles will continue to be "Big Data" and "Clouds", but with an added emphasis on dynamic text and data mining, in other words, on discovering knowledge.

Resilience

Closely related to knowledge discovery is the development of resilience, which is relying on the ability to rapidly detect an attack using the same methods of pattern recognition as in knowledge discovery systems. It is expected that electronic crime, hooliganism (spam and hacking for hacking's sake), terrorism and cyberwars will expand and become real threats for businesses and administrations. This will trigger a wave of activities to develop protection and make digital enterprise resilient.

We have ideas on how to enhance resilience by developing multi-agent immune systems, very similar to the system protecting our organism from infections.

Smart City

There is a huge discrepancy between the city, as it is, and the city as it could be, the Smart City. Just by coordinating management of currently unconnected services and shifting service provision to the Internet, it will be possible to achieve massive savings as well as reduction of pollution.

Whilst the concept of Smart City may be interpreted differently by different participants in the endeavour to built the first prototype, our focus here is purely on managing city resources, and in particular, on managing knowledge as a city resource.

The transformation is likely to proceed stepwise and there will be, hopefully, no attempt to undertake a top-down grand design. However, a *digital smart city infrastructure* is definitely required and it should contain the following elements.

Adaptive Management of Services as a Service

Services for buildings such as cleaning, heating, cooling, ventilation and communication; services for city districts such as cleaning of streets, rubbish collection and street and building maintenance and services for the whole city such as water, gas and electricity supply, communication and drainage, as well as traffic flow will be managed in real time.

Swarms of schedulers will cooperate with each other without being centrally controlled.

Adaptive schedulers for the allocation of resources to demands will be available as a service over the City Net.

City Cloud and City Net

Eventually all relevant data will be housed in the City Cloud and services will be accessible by citizens over the City Net.

We shall be ready to supply multi-agent software for adaptive management of transportation, relevant to a Smart City, i.e., real-time scheduling of ambulances, taxis, share-a-car schemes, rent-a-car operations and retail supply chains as a web-based service. And we are working on some additional ideas, all connected with the IoT, some of which are outlined in the next section.

Smart Parking

Street and building parking spaces are connected to the Internet displaying their availability. Customers, who want to book parking, upload their requirements to dedicated websites. Customer agents and parking agents then negotiate the allocation of parking spaces following our taxi allocation model with delayed commitment, to ensure the best possible allocation.

Smart Heating, Cooling and Ventilation of Large Buildings

The objective is to develop a smart system capable of significantly reducing energy consumption in buildings by anticipating required energy input and maintaining the optimal energy consumption, based on:

- Weather forecasting
- Thermal characteristics of the building
- Patterns of building usage

Key components of the system are:

Knowledge base, which contains (1) knowledge on thermal characteristics of the building and (2) polices on energy consumption.

Weather forecasting module, which receives weather forecasts and information on actual external temperature and extracts relevant information for energy consumption control.

Usage module, which receives usage forecasts and information on actual usage and extracts relevant information for energy consumption control.

Intelligent controller, which makes decisions when to switch on and off the energy taking into account weather forecasting, building usage patterns and thermal characteristics of the building.

Interface, which (1) delivers instructions to switch energy on or off to appropriate actuators and (2) enables energy managers to monitor the system operation and to overrule its decisions, if considered necessary.

Smart Logistics

Disconnected logistic businesses create enormous waste of energy, particularly due to idle runs, and pollution. This book explains why a centralised control of global logistics is not feasible considering complexity of markets, and not desirable. We expect to see instead the development of *digital logistics infrastructure* over large parts of the globe, which will be used by individual logistic businesses to compete and cooperate with each other.

Digital Infrastructure for Logistics

The key elements of the digital infrastructure are:

Dedicated logistics webservices, which collect, display and allocate demands for transportation.

Adaptive planners and schedulers, as a web-based service to be offered to individual logistics businesses and administrations, which plan and schedule the movement of goods and people.

Links to IoT for logistics resources, including trucks, trains, boats, route sections and fuelling points, which enable logistic resources to interact with demands.

Logistics webservices are designed to accept uploads of demands for transport from businesses and individuals, to display these demands and operate MAS handling negotiations between agents of bidders and agents of demands.

Adaptive planners allocate cargoes to different modes of transport, i.e., road, railways and boats, initially based on forecasts and modified, in real time, to accommodate changes in demand as well as route disruptions.

Adaptive schedulers allocate trucks to road sections, trains to railway line sections and boats to river/canna/sea routes.

We have many ideas that could be incorporated into digital infrastructure for logistics, as exemplified by the two proposals given in the following sections.

Smart Parcels

Parcels containing, say, spare parts for aircraft contain in their electronic tags information about their size, weight, content, destination and amount of credit, which they are allowed to spend on transport and storage fees. They are connected to the Internet and their senders can at any time during their journey change instructions about their destination.

If, indeed, the destination where spare parts are needed, changes, parcel agents will renegotiate new transport arrangements directly with airline agents and pay the fees for extra storage time, if any, agreed with warehouse agents, and for new fares, agreed with airline agents, into appropriate accounts.

Smart Aircraft Servicing

Numerous sensors, built into important components of aircraft, collect information on their performance and, if deterioration is detected, upload this information to the Internet. The servicing unit located at the aircraft destination monitors broadcasts from aircraft sensors over the Internet, and if a need for repair or component replacement is detected, wakes up aircraft agent. The agent consults ontology to find out what is necessary to do and starts negotiations with appropriate resource agents aimed at producing a schedule for service engineers, tools and spare parts to be available at the appropriate location when aircraft lands.

The story of managing complexity

This book tells you a story of managing complexity.

Let's summarise it:

"*Complexity* of the world in which we live and work is relentlessly increasing.

To prosper under conditions of complexity we need to learn how to *manage complexity*, which means *coping with external complexity* and *tuning internal complexity*.

The best way of coping with complexity is to become *adaptive* and to allocate resources to demands as they change, in real time.

The first step towards adaptability is to change one's *mindset*, which means to feel comfortable with uncertainty, to be satisfied with the best possible solution obtainable in the available time (rather than to seek the impossible – the optimum), to appreciate power of self-organisation, to accept that the world evolves irreversibly and that outcomes of this process are unpredictable. And above all, to look for opportunities where others see only danger.

The second step is to develop an *adaptive strategy* and then to design and implement *adaptive resource allocation systems*. Adaptability requires monitoring of large quantity of data, dynamic forecasting of changes in demands and resources, and rapid, real-time, decision-making when reacting to frequent disruptive events, and therefore cannot be achieved without employing appropriate technology, such as *multi-agent software*.

Key issues in managing complexity are *resolving conflicts by negotiations*, rather than optimising, reacting in real time to any change as it happens, rather than waiting for data to accumulate for batch processing and *continuously improving current solutions*."

The story is illustrated with many examples of businesses, which required help for coping with complexity, became adaptive, immediately improved performance and, unknowingly, contributed to this story.

Knowledge behind the story did not exist when we began this venture. We learned as we delivered adaptive systems to our clients and as we learned we organised new knowledge as a story.

We wrote and rewrote the story as we attempted to resolve the important conflict created by:

1. Pressure to deliver to clients the best possible service within tight deadlines and limited budget (we are both devoted entrepreneurs)

2. Intense curiosity to discover and formulate knowledge on how to manage complexity (we are both devoted researchers, too).

We now have new knowledge on how to manage complexity, formulated as a story and corroborated in practice. You can learn from this book and design adaptive systems, and then learn from your experience and compose an improved story, *your story*.

References

[1] Prigogine, I., *The End of Certainty: Time, Chaos and the New Laws of Nature*, Free Press, ISBN 0-684-83705-6, 1997.

[2] Prigogine, I., *Is Future Given?* World Scientific Publishing Co., 2003.

[3] Kaufman, S., *At Home in the Universe: The Search for the Laws of Self-Organization and Complexity*, Oxford Press, ISBN 0-19-511130-3, 1995.

[4] Holland, J.H., *Hidden Order: How Adaptation Builds Complexity*, Addison Wesley, 1995.

[5] Holland, J., *Emergence: From Chaos to Order*, Oxford University Press, ISBN 0-19850409-8, 1998.

[6] Schumacher, E.F., *Small Is Beautiful: A Study of Economics as if People Mattered*, Harper Collins, ISBN 0-349-13137-6, 1974.

[7] Rzevski, G., Investigating current social, economic and educational issues using framework and tools of complexity science. *Journal of the World University Forum*, **1(2)**, ISSN 1835-2030, pp. 75–84, 2008.

[8] Rzevski, G., A practical methodology for managing complexity. *Emergence: Complexity & Organization – An International Transdisciplinary Journal of Complex Social Systems*, **13(1–2)**, ISSN 1521-3250, pp. 38–56, 2011.

[9] Beinhocker, E., *The Origin of Wealth: Evolution, Complexity and the Radical Remaking of Economics*, Random House Business Books, ISBN 978-0-712-67661-8, 2007.

[10] Rzevski, G., Using tools of complexity science to diagnose the current financial crisis. *Optoelectronics, Instrumentation and Data Processing*, **46(2)**, ISSN 8756-6990, 2010.

[11] Taleb, N.N., *The Black Swan: The Impact of the Highly Improbable*, Penguin Books, 2007.

[12] Dekker, S., *Drift into Failure*, Kindle edition, Amazon, 2012.

[13] Kuhn, T., *The Structure of Scientific Revolutions*, Second edition, Enlarged, The University of Chicago Press, ISBN 0-226-45804-0, 1970.

[14] Drucker, P., *The Age of Discontinuity*, Harper Row, 1969.

[15] Rzevski, G., Skobelev, P., Batishchev, S. & Orlov, A., A framework for multi-agent modelling of virtual organisations. *Processes and Foundations for Virtual Organisations*, eds. L.M. Camarinha-Matos & H. Afsarmanesh, Kluwer Academic Publishers, ISBN 978-1-4020-7638-1, pp. 253–260, 2003.

[16] Anderson, C., *The Long Tail: How Endless Choice Is Creating Unlimited Demand*, Random House Business Books, ISBN 1-8441-3850-X, 2006.

[17] Surowiecki, J., *The Wisdom of Crowds*, Abacus, ISBN 0-349-11605-9, 2004.

[18] Lanham, R., *The Economy of Attention*, The University of Chicago Press, ISBN 978-0-226-46867-9, 2007.

[19] Rzevski, G., Skobelev, P., Minakov, I. & Volman, S., Dynamic pattern discovery using multi-agent technology. *Proc. of the 6th WSEAS Int. Conf. On Telecommunications and Informatics (TELE_INFO '07)*, Dallas, TX, ISBN 978-9-6084-5760-7, pp. 75–81, 2007.

[20] Minakov, I., Rzevski, G., Skobelev, P. & Volman, S., Creating contract templates for car insurance using multi-agent based text understanding and clustering. *Lecture Notes in*

Computer Science, Volume 4659, Holonic and Multi-Agent Systems for Manufacturing. Third Int. Conf. On Industrial Applications of Holonic and Multi-Agent Systems, HoloMAS 2007, Springer: Regensburg, Germany, ISBN 978-3-54074478-8, pp. 361–371, 2007.

[21] Rzevski, G. & Skobelev, P., *Agent Based Semantic Web*, Semantic Universe Website, 2009.

[22] Hettige, B., Karunananda, A.S. & Rzevski, G., Multi agent framework for development of machine translation systems. *8th Int. Conf. On Science & Education ICCSE 2013*, Colombo, Sri Lanka, 2013.

[23] Rzevski, G., Using complexity science framework and multi-agent technology in design. *Embracing Complexity in Design*, eds. K. Alexiou, J. Johnson & T. Zamenopoulos, Routledge, ISBN 978-0-4154-9700-8, pp. 61–72, 2010.

[24] Rzevski, G., Multi-agent technology for designing adaptive business processes. *Proc. of the 12th IEEE/ACIS Int. Conf. On Computer and Information Science (ICIS 2013)*, Niigata, Japan, ISBN 978-1-4799-0172-2, pp. 83–89, 2013.

[25] Madsen, B., Skobelev, P., Rzevski, G. & Tsarev, A., Real-time multi-agent forecasting and replenishment solution for LEGOs branded retail outlets. *International Journal of Software Innovation*, **1(2)**, ISSN 2166-7100, pp. 28–39, IGI Global, 2013.

[26] Kapitza, S., Global population blow-up and after: the demographic revolution and information society. *Report to the Club of Rome*, ISBN 3-98-097235-6, 2006.

[27] Rzevski, G (ed.), *Mechatronics: Designing Intelligent Machines*, Butterworth Heinemann, ISBN 0-7506-2404-3, 1995.

[28] Newell, A. & Simon, H.A. *GPS, a Program That Simulates Human Thoughts* ed. H. Billing, Lernende Automaten, pp. 109–124, 1961.

[29] Feigenbaum, E.A., Buchanan, B.G. & Lederberg, J., On generality and problem solving: a case study using the DENDRAL program, ed. B. Meltzer & D. Michie, *Machine Intelligence*, **6**, pp. 165–190, 1971.

[30] McDermot, J., R1: A rule-based configurer of computer systems. *Artificial Intelligence*, **19(1)**, pp. 39–88, 1982.

[31] Rumelhart, D.E. & McClleland, J.L. (eds), *Parallel Distributed Processing*, MIT Press: Cambridge, 1986.

[32] Rzevski, G. & Skobelev, P., Emergent intelligence in large scale multi-agent systems. *International Journal of Education and Information Technology*, **1(2)**, pp. 64–71, 2007.

[33] Minsky, M., *The Society of Mind*, Heinemann, ISBN 0-43-446758-8, 1985.

[34] Edelman, G., *Bright Air. Brilliant Fire. On the Matter of the Mind*, Allen Lane the Penguin Press: London, ISBN 0-713-99096-1, 1992.

[35] Noble, D., *The Music of Life*, Oxford University Press, ISBN 0-19-929573-5, 2006.

[36] Kozhevnikov, S., Larukhin, V. & Skobelev, P., Smart enterprise: multi-agent solution for Holonic enterprise resource management. *Proc. of the 12th IEEE/ACIS Int. Conf. On Computer and Information Science (ICIS 2013)*, Niigata, Japan, ISBN 978-1-4799-0172-2, 2013.

[37] Nicolis, G. & Prigogine, I., *Exploring Complexity*, W.H. Freeman, ISBN 0-7167-1859-6, 1939.

[38] Popper, K., *Conjectures and Refutations: The Growth of Scientific Knowledge*. Rutledge & Kegan Paul Ltd: London, ISBN 0-7100-6508-6, 1963.

[39] Glaschenko, A., Ivaschenko, A., Rzevski, G. & Skobelev, P., Multi-agent real time scheduling system for taxi companies. *Proc. of the 8th Int. Conf. On Autonomous Agents and Multiagent Systems (AAMAS 2009)*, eds. Decker, Sichman, Sierra & Castelfranchi, Budapest, Hungary, ISBN 978-0-98173816-1, pp. 29–35, 2009.

[40] Andreev, S., Rzevski, G., Shveykin, P., Skobelev, P. & Yankov, I., Multi-agent scheduler for rent-a-car companies. *Lecture Notes in Computer Science, Volume 5696, Holonic and Multi-Agent Systems for Manufacturing: Forth Int. Conf. On Industrial Applications of Holonic and Multi-Agent Systems*, HoloMAS, Springer: Linz, Austria, ISBN 978-3-5407-4478-8, pp. 305–314, 2009.

[41] Himoff, J., Rzevski, G. & Skobelev, P., Magenta technology: multi-agent logistics i-scheduler for road transportation. *International Conference on Autonomous Agents: Proc. of the 5th Int. Joint Conf. On Autonomous Agents and Multi-Agent Systems*, Hakodate, Japan, ISBN 1-59-593303-4, pp. 1541–1521, 2006.

[42] Ivashenko, A., Khamits, I., Skobelev, P. & Sychova, M. Multi-agent system for scheduling of flight program, cargo flow and resources of international space station. *5th Int. Conf. On Industrial Applications of Holonic and Multi-Agent Systems (HoloMAS 2011)*, Springer Verlag: France, Toulouse, pp. 165–174, 2011.

[43] Gilaev, A., Sollogub, A., Skobelev, P., Simonova, E., Stepanov, M. & Tsarev, A., Smart multi-agent system for distributed control of satellites for distant observation of Earth. *Information and Control Systems*, **1(62)**, pp. 16–26, 2013.

[44] Shabunin, A., Kuznetsov, N., Skobelev, P., Babanin, I., Stepanov, M. & Simonova, E., Multi-agent system for railways resource management. *Mechatronics, Automation, Control*, 1, pp. 23–29, 2013.

[45] Tyrin, I., Andrey Vylegzhanin, Elina Kolbova, Oleg Kuznetzov, Petr Skobelev, Alexander Tsarev, Yaroslav Shepilov, Multi-agent system "smart factory" for real-time workshop management: results of design & implementation for Izhevsk axion-holding factory. *Pro. of 2012 IEEE 17th Int. Conf. On Emerging Technologies & Factory Automation (ETFA 2012)*, Krakow, Poland, 4 pp., 2012, http://www.etfa2012.org/

[46] Shpilevoy, V., Shishov, A., Skobelev, P., Kolbova, E., Kazanskaia, D., Shepilov, Ya. & Tsarev, A., Multi-agent system "smart factory" for real-time workshop management in aircraft jet engines production. *Proc. of the 11th IFAC Workshop on Intelligent Manufacturing Systems (IMS'13)*, São Paulo, Brazil, 2013.

[47] Granichin, O., Petr Skobelev, Alexander Lada, Igor Mayorov & Alexander Tsarev, Cargo transportation models analysis using multi-agent adaptive real-time truck scheduling system. *Proc. of 5th Int. Conf. On Agents and Artificial Intelligence (ICAART'2013)*, Barcelona, Spain, SciTePress: Portugal, Vol. 2, pp. 244–249, ISBN 978-9-8985-6539-6, 2013.

[48] Blinov, S., Serduk, V., Onischenko, G., Laruchin, V., Ochkov, D., Skobelev, P. & Tsarev, A., Multi-agent system for managing mobile teams for Samara region gas distributor. *Proc. of the Int. Conf. On Complex Systems*, Samara, Russia, pp. 64–69, 2013.

[49] Vittikh, V.A., Larukhin, V.B. & Tsarev, A.V., Actors, Holonic enterprises, ontologies and multi-agent technology. *Proc. of the Int. Conf. On Holonic and Multi-Agent Systems in Manufacturing (HoloMAS 2013), Lecture Notes in Artificial Intelligence*, **8062**, eds. V. Marik, M. Lastra & P. Skobelev, Springer Verlag: Prague, Czech Republic, pp. 13–24, 2013.

Authors

Prof. George Rzevski is an academic, entrepreneur and consultant based in London, UK.

He is Professor Emeritus, Complexity Science and Design Research Group at The Open University, Milton Keynes, UK.

George served as Visiting Professor at London School of Economics; Brunel University, West London; Wuhan University, China; Cologne University of Applied Sciences, Germany; and Moratuwa University, Colombo, Sri Lanka.

George and Petr are Joint Founders of a network of advanced technology companies, which include Magenta Corporation, London, UK, and Samara, Russia; Rzevski Solutions Ltd, London; Knowledge Genesis Ltd, London, UK, and Hanover, Germany; Smart Solutions Ltd, Samara; and Multi-Agent Technology Ltd, London, UK.

The companies are engaged in marketing and developing multi-agent systems for adaptive allocation of resources (complexity management) and the network is self-organising to adapt to changing market conditions.

Until 1999 George was a full-time academic and Professor in Department of Design and Innovation at The Open University, Milton Keynes, where he was Director, Centre for the Design of Intelligent Systems. His Centre was well funded by grants from government and industry and his Department was rated 5 out of 5 in the two UK Research Assessment Exercises.

As a tribute to his successful research career, the University established recently a new "The George Rzevski Complexity Laboratory".

At The Open University George pioneered undergraduate education in intelligent mechatronics launching a course in which each of 400 students were given his/her personal intelligent robot to conduct experiments at home.

Prof. Rzevski has published widely and delivered keynote papers at numerous international conferences. Jointly with Petr, George has three UK and international patents on multi-agent systems for logistics, dynamic data mining and semantic processing.

He supervised a large number of PhD projects and acted as external examiner for undergraduate and postgraduate courses in many UK university departments. He served as editor-in-chief of the *Journal of Artificial Intelligence in Engineering*, published by Elsevier.

He has assessed candidates for tenure on behalf of a number of American universities, including Stamford, Ohio and Texas; examined over 30 PhD students from universities in the UK and abroad, including Cambridge University, Imperial College, LSE, Royal College of Art, The Open University, Cardiff University, Singapore University and National University of Ireland.

For several years George has delivered a regular series of lectures on Economic, Social and Cultural Implications of Global Networks to postgraduate students at London School of Economics.

Throughout his academic career George worked as a consultant for private companies, government administrations and EU on various issues related to advanced information technologies. He has advised ITT Communications, London, Antwerp and Paris; ICL Computers, Manchester; IBM, London; Philips, Eindhoven.

He began his academic career in the UK at Kingston Polytechnic, later Kingston University, where he was Professor and Founder Head of Information Systems. At Kingston he launched new undergraduate and postgraduate courses aimed at bringing together disciplines of Information Technology (IT) and Business and led a successful research centre in Computer-Integrated Manufacturing. The Centre worked in close cooperation with leading high-technology companies, including ICL, Xerox and IBM.

George is of Russian origin. His family emigrated from Russia in 1918 and settled in Serbia, where he was born in 1932 and educated at the University of Belgrade. In his late twenties he was given an opportunity to establish a new design office in Belgrade. He hand-picked his staff employing only talented young engineers and the design bureaux grew under his leadership into a major organisation capable of undertaking large-scale electrical engineering projects. At the age of 29 George was Chief Designer of all major railways electrification schemes in Yugoslavia.

George moved to the UK in the 1960s where he attended a postgraduate refresher course at Imperial College before joining Kingston.

Prof. Petr Skobelev is Founder, President and Product/Technology Leader of the software engineering company Smart Solutions Ltd in Samara, Russia, and focused on developing multi-agent technology and solutions. He is also Director and Co-owner, with George, of Multi-Agent Technology Ltd, London, UK.

Petr has graduated from Computer Science Department of Samara Aerospace University in 1983 and obtained PhD degree in Functional Programming Languages and Artificial Intelligence for Aerospace Applications in 1986. Petr is Senior Researcher at the Institute of Control of Complex Systems of Russian Academy of Science and Professor of Multi-Agent Systems at the Volga Region Academy of Telecommunications and Informatics, Samara State Aerospace University and State University of Railways.

Between 1983 and 1991 Petr Skobelev was senior scientist and chief developer of real-time measurement and control systems, image processing systems, intelligent simulators and expert systems for Samara Branch of Institute of Physics and Institute of Complex System of Russian Academy of Science.

At the beginning of Perestroika, in 1990, he met George and they started collaborative research and design projects in the area of multi-agent systems. This collaboration led to Petr's intense entrepreneurial activity. He started his first business, ArtLog Ltd, in Samara, developing intelligent tutoring systems and learning environments and then, in 1997, Knowledge Genesis Ltd, also in Samara, a software house specialising in multi-agent e-Government applications.

In 1999, George and Petr founded Magenta Corporation Ltd in London, UK, with a software development branch in Samara, the company that is still successfully developing multi-agent software for large-scale industrial applications. The partnership worked rather well and after they left Magenta Corporation, they expanded to Germany and the USA and considerably increased the UK and Russian business, transferring it to Multi-Agent Technology Ltd and Smart Solutions Ltd, respectively.

All commercial applications described in the book have been developed under Petr's direct supervision in Samara.

In 2012 Smart Solutions has won IP project in FP7 EU Program "Smart Factories" together with EADS and Airbus, Cologne University, Prague University,

Manchester University, Politechnik Institute of Braganca and partners from other countries.

In 2013 Smart Solutions has been recognised as one of the most innovative and fast growing companies in Russia. The award was given by the Association of Innovative Regions in Russia and Russian Venturing Company. The assessment was performed by PricewaterhouseCoopers.

Petr's research interests include multi-agent platforms and applications as well as emergent intelligence. He authored more than 150 publications and, jointly with George, has three UK and international patents on multi-agent systems for logistics, dynamic data mining and semantic processing.

He is member of IEEE IES Technical Committee on Industrial Agents (http://tcia.ieee-ies.org/).

Index

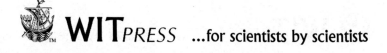

Mobile Agents

Principles of Operation and Applications

Edited by: A. GENCO, University of Palermo, Italy

Multi-agent systems are one of the most effective software design paradigms, and they are considered to be the most recent evolutionary step of object-oriented programming. Agents have several advantages when compared with objects. The most important among them is that they are made of active code, which is capable of acting autonomously.

Agents can be a suitable choice to exploit the Internet reality since users can operate easily in a less compelling way and also reduce Internet connection time. Mobile agents thus make a PC an intelligent entity able to autonomously accomplish tasks boring to humans, starting from document search up to actual business negotiations. Mobile agents allow human owners to decide if and when their intervention is suitable or required.

The book describes the mobile agent principles of operation in detail. It starts by giving some definitions, and illustrates their main features, such as mobility, communication, coordination, interoperability, fault tolerance and security. Comparisons of these features between most relevant multi-agent developing platforms are then discussed. The book ends with a discussion on a mobile agent application field, namely data mining and information retrieval, thus showing how mobile agents can help us to face these field-related problems.

Series: Advances in Management Information, Vol 6
ISBN: 978-1-84564-060-6   eISBN: 978-1-84564-297-6
Published 2008 / 304pp / £109.00

WIT Press is a major publisher of engineering research. The company prides itself on producing books by leading researchers and scientists at the cutting edge of their specialities, thus enabling readers to remain at the forefront of scientific developments. Our list presently includes monographs, edited volumes, books on disk, and software in areas such as: Acoustics, Advanced Computing, Architecture and Structures, Biomedicine, Boundary Elements, Earthquake Engineering, Environmental Engineering, Fluid Mechanics, Fracture Mechanics, Heat Transfer, Marine and Offshore Engineering and Transport Engineering.

WITPRESS   ...for scientists by scientists

Grid Technologies

Emerging from Distributed Architectures to Virtual Organisations

*Edited by: **M.P. BEKAKOS** and **G.A. GRAVVANIS**, Democritus University of Thrace, Greece and **H.R. ARABNIA**, The University of Georgia, USA*

Grid Computing is a new emerging research area that promotes the development and advancement of technologies that provide seamless and scalable access to wide-area distributed resources.

Current grid-enabling technologies consist of stand-alone architectures. A typical architecture provides middleware access to various services at different hierarchical levels. Computational Grids enable the sharing, selection and aggregation of a wide variety of geographically distributed computation resources (such as supercomputers, clusters of computers, storage systems, data sources, instruments, people, etc.) and present them as a single unified resource for solving large-scale computations and data intensive computing applications (e.g. engineering problems, molecular modelling for drug design, brain activity analysis, high energy physics, etc.)

This book is an excellent reference for the realisation and use of various grid technology issues. The book is divided into two parts of self-standing chapters, each part surveying several subjects of interest in the areas of web services, middleware, and distributed and grid computing methodologies. It contains a significant amount of expository and explanatory material that is structured in a modular fashion, with working experts describing their implementation research, including results.

The book, as text and research material, is aimed at graduate/postgraduate students and researchers working in the area of grid technologies. It can also be used by educators at these levels to illustrate the use and methods of grid computing.

Series: Advances in Management Information, Vol 5
ISBN: 978-1-84564-055-2   eISBN: 978-1-84564-258-7
Published 2006 / 512pp / £206.00

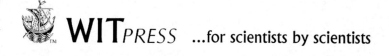
Coevolutionary Computation and Multiagent Systems

L. JIAO, J. LIU and W. ZHONG, Xidian University, China

The origins of evolutionary computation can be traced back to the late 1950s where it remained, almost unknown to the broader scientific community, for three decades until the 1980s, when it started to receive significant attention, as did the study of multi-agent systems (MAS). This volume focuses on systems in which many intelligent agents interact with each other. Today these systems are not simply a research topic but are also beginning to become an important subject of academic teaching and industrial and commercial application. *Coevolutionary Computation and Multiagent Systems* introduces the authors' recent work in these two new and important branches of artificial intelligence.

ISBN: 978-1-84564-638-7   eISBN: 978-1-84564-639-4
Published 2012 / 270pp / £129.00

Text Mining and its Applications to Intelligence, CRM and Knowledge Management

Edited by: A. ZANASI, TEMIS Text Mining Solutions SA, Italy

Organisations generate and collect large volumes of textual data. Unfortunately, many companies are unable to capitalise fully on the value of this data because information implicit within it is not easy to discern. Primarily intended for business analysts and statisticians across multiple industries, this book provides an introduction to the types of problems encountered and currently available text mining solutions.

Partial Contents: Text Processing and Information Retrieval; Application Integration in Applied Text Mining; ROI in Text Mining Projects; Open Sources Automatic Analysis for Corporate and Government Intelligence; Customer Feedbacks and Opinion Surveys Analysis in the Automotive Industry; Text Mining Based Knowledge Management in Banking; Text Mining in Life Sciences; Link Analysis in Crime Pattern Detection.

Series: Advances in Management Information Vol 2
ISBN: 978-1-85312-995-7   ISBN-10: 1-85312-995-X
Published 2005 / 368pp+CD / £183.00

Lightning Source UK Ltd.
Milton Keynes UK
UKOW04n1428170314

228263UK00001B/4/P